OLIVES LEMONS & ZA'ATAR

Rawia Bishara opened her restaurant Tanoreen in Bay Ridge, Brooklyn in 1998. *New York Magazine* has named it the best Mezze and #1 Cheap Eats. *The New York Times, Gourmet* magazine, *The New Yorker, The Village Voice, Travel & Leisure, Zagat Restaurant Survey, Michelin Guides, Time Out New York, The New York Post* and Food Network's 'The Best Thing I Ever Ate' have all featured or positively reviewed Tanoreen. Rawia has had her recipes published in *The New York Times, New York Magazine* and *Plate Magazine* and teaches a recurring class at DeGustibus Culinary School in New York City.

OLIVES
LEMONS
& ZA'ATAR

THE BEST MIDDLE EASTERN HOME COOKING

RAWIA BISHARA

PHOTOGRAPHY BY PETER CASSIDY

KYLE BOOKS

DEDICATION

To my mother and father, Monira and Anton,
for sharing a love of food, family and the value
of togetherness around our dinner table.

First published in Great Britain in 2014
by Kyle Books, an imprint of Kyle Cathie Ltd.
192–198 Vauxhall Bridge Road
London, SW1V 1DX
general.enquiries@kylebooks.com
www.kylebooks.co.uk

10

ISBN: 978-0-85783-230-6

Text © 2014 by Rawia Bishara and Jumana Bishara
Photography © 2014 by Peter Cassidy, except the photographs
on page 219, courtesy of Rawia Bishara
Book design © 2014 by Kyle Cathie Ltd

Project editors Anja Schmidt and Vicki Murrell
Designer Paul Palmer-Edwards and Louise Evans
at Grade Design
Photographer Peter Cassidy
Food styling Linda Tubby
Prop styling Iris Bromet
Copy editor Sarah Scheffel
Production by Nic Jones, Gemma John and Lisa Pinnell

A Cataloguing in Publication record for this title is available
from the British Library

Colour reproduction by ALTA, London
Printed and bound in China by C&C Offset Printing Co., Ltd.

CONTENTS

INTRODUCTION

Rawia, in Arabic, means storyteller. But rather than narrate the stories about my family, life and culture, I prefer to tell them through my cooking. In my mind, how ingredients are procured, dishes are served and meals are celebrated speak volumes.

I was born into a food-loving Palestinian-Arab family in Nazareth, a beautiful town in southern Galilee. Though the words 'organic', 'locavore' and 'sustainable' were unknown then, my parents' approach to food and cooking qualified on all counts. They were 'foodies' before the word was coined. And so were their parents before them.

My grandmother always had several ceramic urns filled with fruity olive oil, pressed from the olives my aunts and uncles picked on her family's land. My mother, too, made her own olive oil, and used the remaining 'crude' to make soap. She also distilled her own vinegar, sun-dried herbs and fruits, made batches of goats' cheese as well as fermented sweet wine, and jarred jewel-coloured jams from the bounty of the local orchards.

I have endless food memories from my childhood, but the most vivid are the summers I spent with my four brothers and sisters at our grandparents' homes in the villages of Rama and Tarshiha in the hills of Galilee. The drive from Nazareth was itself a food lover's dream. A colourful mosaic of rooftops stretched into the horizon, each one laden with vegetables and herbs drying in the sun. There were plum tomatoes, aubergines, okra, smoked wheat, sesame seeds, za'atar, sumac, figs, apricots and spearmint – a mouthwatering bounty that would be stored for winter cooking and eating. We returned from our July sojourn with enough food to yield meal after delicious meal for months. This was my childhood; this was how I came to respect where and how food is grown and prepared.

FROM NAZARETH TO NEW YORK

When I married my husband, Wafa, and moved to Bay Ridge in Brooklyn, New York, I found myself immersed in one of the most multicultural regions on earth. I was so enthralled with the diverse cuisines that I practically ate my way through the city. These forays influenced my cooking very dramatically.

'I HAVE DOZENS OF FOND FOOD MEMORIES FROM MY CHILDHOOD, BUT THE MOST VIVID HAS LONG REMAINED THE SUMMERS I SPENT WITH MY FOUR BROTHERS AND SISTERS AT OUR GRANDPARENTS' HOME IN TARSHIHA IN THE HILLS OF GALILEE.'

In the years that followed, my husband and I planned international family trips with our daughter, Jumana, and son, Tarek, which further broadened my culinary repertoire. I will never forget one summer trip to Spain in particular, during which I bribed my children into sharing paella at least once a day, so to experience that national dish in all its variations. That food experience in turn influenced how I prepare my version of *sayadiyya*, the traditional Middle Eastern fisherman's dish.

Our European trips were special, but none quite compared to the visits we regularly took back home to the Middle East. It was important to me that my children not only understood their heritage, but that they connected to Middle Eastern food the way I did as a child.

When my children were grown and on their own, I started to work and became the head of a women's organisation in New York that assisted recent immigrants with their integration into American life. The job involved a lot of entertaining, a role I loved, and my co-workers constantly urged me to open a restaurant, as did friends and family for whom I had been cooking for years. It became clear to me that I needed to take the leap.

CREATING TANOREEN

In 1998, I opened my restaurant, Tanoreen, as a tribute to my mother, Monira Hanna, and to reinterpret her imaginative Middle Eastern cooking. She was an impressive and enthusiastic cook who whipped together meals for the seven us – and often many guests who gathered around our table – most nights of the week. Though she was inspired by the cooking traditions of her native Galilee, her approach was not rigidly authentic. She understood the value of bending the

rules when it came to cooking, a practise we relished at the dinner table. I adored this about her and strive every day to enliven my life – and my food – with the kind of creative flourishes that defined my mother's life.

Tanoreen is named after a majestic village located in the northern valleys of Lebanon. It is so beautiful that it inspired the iconic Middle Eastern singer, Fairuz, to record an ode to it. The origin of the word is derived from *tannour*, a stone oven used in ancient times, but, to be honest, I also like that it is easy to pronounce, unlike my name, which I have spent my whole life spelling and pronouncing for people!

Initially I opened Tanoreen in a modest storefront with only twelve tables. The menu featured staples such as simple sandwiches, spreads and salads. However, I quickly established a loyal clientele and learned that what they enjoyed the most was the homestyle cooking closest to my heart. They loved the dishes I had learned to cook from my mother, the meals that have consistently been a source of joy in my life.

An ever-evolving menu combined with happy customers and good word of mouth led to some positive reviews in notable publications. Before I knew it, lines were forming around the block. I needed to expand, and ten years after opening my little restaurant, I made it grow. We bought a property nearby and opened a much larger restaurant, seating 40 to 50 tables, as well as keeping a take-away counter round the back.

EMBRACING CHANGE AND MIXING IT UP

My cooking celebrates tradition and embraces change. In some instances, I recreate dishes as they have been made for generations; other times, I experiment a bit, making a recipe more contemporary by adding a few more spices or offering a few shortcuts. The most popular examples are my Brussels sprouts, prepared with panko and tahini; a lamb shank marinated in herbs and rose buds; a kafta roll (a reconstructed classic); and an aubergine Napoleon made with baba ghanouj layered between crisp aubergine and topped with basil and tomatoes – all of which you'll find in these pages.

My commitment to ingredients, respect for my heritage and passion for cooking come together in the following chapters. You will find creative, flavourful yet traditional recipes, enlivened for the modern cook. My version of Middle Eastern food is unique and distinguished by its subtlety, variety, balance and accessibility.

'TRUTH BE TOLD, MIDDLE EASTERN CUISINE STRETCHES GALAXIES BEYOND FALAFEL AND SHISH KEBABS. THE FOOD I COOK IS JUST AS VARIED AS, SAY, ITALIAN CUISINE – THE DISHES ARE A REFLECTION OF GEOGRAPHY, CLIMATE AND AGRICULTURE.'

Often when new customers dine at Tanoreen they are surprised by the unique flavours and range of dishes we serve. Truth be told, Middle Eastern cuisine stretches galaxies beyond falafel and shish kebabs. The food I cook is just as varied as, say, Italian cuisine – the dishes are a reflection of geography, climate and agriculture.

None of these are complicated chef's recipes but rather, a collection from the heart, an account of a life set in two culinary worlds with recipes that I've created from both my head and my heart. While I have resolute respect for the culinary rites and rituals of my native Israel, you will notice that I like to mix it up a bit in ways that veer from tradition. I learned the beauty of doing this from the best – my mother. She never approached cooking as a technical endeavour – following recipes to the letter or strictly adhering to measures. She did, however, cook with an abundance of love. I tend to use spices very liberally and love the tang that an ample amount of lemon juice adds to a dish. Season your food to your liking, and enjoy the process of preparing it for the people you love. Cooking is so very personal – use your imagination, intuition, heart and, most importantly, your taste buds! My hope is that the recipes you find here will not only bring you great satisfaction in the kitchen, but will help you create an atmosphere of conviviality and hospitality – an essential part of the pleasure of cooking and eating.

STORECUPBOARD

Allspice: This is a ground, dried berry (not a mixture of spices as its name suggests), used frequently in the Levant. It features notes of cinnamon, nutmeg and cloves.

✤ Tip: use this on lamb especially, as it eliminates the 'gamey' flavour.

Basmati rice: This long-grain rice has a soft texture and nutty flavour. In Arabic, 'basmati' means 'my smile'.

Black pepper: This ubiquitous ground spice is used in all my dishes to add a base flavour element.

✤ Tip: Grind peppercorns fresh to achieve the optimum taste.

Bulgur wheat: This high-fibre whole grain is used throughout the Middle East for soups, salads and main dishes. It comes in various sizes from whole to fine. For example, the bulgur we use in Tabbouleh (page 73) is a smaller grain than for Kibbeh (page 35).

✤ Tip: It's a great substitute for rice in Vegetarian Vine Leaves (page 49).

Cardamom: This spice pod is something we grind into our own Tanoreen spice blend. We use cardamom in savoury dishes, desserts and even grind a few pods with our coffee.

✤ Tip: Open a pod and chew on the seeds to instantly freshen your breath.

Cinnamon: This spice is derived from a particular tree bark and was imported to Egypt as early as 2000 BC. It's uniquely 'sweet' in aroma but can be added to many Middle Eastern dishes as a savoury seasoning as well.

✤ Tip: Sprinkle sparingly over a plain rice pilaf for an instant flavour boost.

Chilli paste: I prefer Middle Eastern chilli pastes to all others; the Turkish seedless brands are fantastic. You can find them in most Middle Eastern shops or online.

Citric acid: Found in most citrus fruits, this 'sour salt' adds a concentrated, lemony flavour, without adding the additional juice. It's also used in cheese and wine production.

✤ Tip: Since it looks exactly like salt, but with a slightly larger crystal structure, take care not to mix these up!

Coriander seed: This antioxidant-rich, intensely flavoured seed of the coriander plant is ground into a powder and used in many of our dishes.

✤ Tip: Throw a few coriander seeds in with your pickling brine to give great flavour.

Cumin: This seed is famous for its distinctive smoky/nutty flavour. It's used in cuisines around the world, stretching from Mexico to Italy to India and beyond. Surprisingly, it's a member of the parsley family. In the old days it was used to alleviate stomach upset, which is why it is traditionally used in grain dishes.

✤ Tip: Cumin boiled with ginger makes a great digestive tea.

Freekeh: Freekeh is smoked green wheat berries. It has a smoky aroma and a nutty, toasted flavour. The green wheat hull is placed over an open flame during which the straw is burned off, leaving behind a unique flavour.

✤ Tip: Freekeh can be used instead of rice to stuff chicken or in soups and stews.

Ghee: Ghee is clarified, evaporated butter. After butter is melted and simmered long enough to evaporate, the moisture becomes richer in flavour than oil and has a higher smoking point than butter.

✤ Tip: Ghee keeps at room temperature for several weeks and for months in the fridge. You can make your our own or buy it in most ethnic food shops or online.

Lentils: This legume has been cultivated since antiquity. After soy beans, they have the highest protein content of any vegetable and are also packed with fibre.

✤ Tip: We usually use red lentils for soups, as I find them more tender.

Maftool: A pasta traditionally made by hand-rolling flour around wheat berries to make pearl-sized grains that are then steamed in chicken broth. Packaged maftool is available in most Middle Eastern markets.

Mahlab: A spice made from the seeds of the St. Lucy's cherry, mahlab gives a subtle floral taste to desserts.

Mastic: A plant resin with a somewhat piney flavour, liquid mastic is dried into small hardened chunks that are crushed into a powder before being added to a recipe. Mastic gives Sahleb (page 202) its unique flavour.

Nutmeg: A strong, slightly sweet spice from the nutmeg tree, this is best freshly grated.

Olive oil: For fresh salads, drizzling or quick sautéing, we recommend using only the extra virgin variety. You can use a lighter variety for cooking.

✤ Tip: Experiment with different kinds of olive oil, as Spanish olive oil is different in flavour and colour from Italian or Greek varieties. Some are sweeter and some more peppery.

Orange blossom water: Orange blossom water is the distilled essence of the orange blossom flower. It's intensely floral and excellent in desserts.

✤ Tip: Boil water and add a few drops of orange blossom water to make a great digestive 'white tea', or add some to fresh mint lemonade.

Pomegranate molasses: Made from the seeds of the pomegranate fruit, this thick, sweet syrup imparts a perfect sweet-sour note into many Middle Eastern dishes.

✤ Tip: Drizzle this into salad dressings, make it into a sorbet or pour some into a cocktail.

Red chilli paste (harissa): Harissa is a combination of chilli, garlic, coriander (and/or cumin) and some olive oil. You can substitute your own chilli paste with the above ingredients if it's not readily available.

✤ Tip: Spread some on a sandwich or spoon it in soup to spice up the flavour factor.

Rose water: Distilled from rose petals, this aromatic ingredient adds a unique flavour to Middle Eastern desserts.

✤ Tip: As it has a very strong flavour and aroma, start with a small amount and add more to taste.

Sesame seeds: I suggest purchasing these raw and dry-roasting them until golden brown so you get the full flavour punch. They quickly turn rancid, so store them in your freezer.

✤ Tip: High in calcium, iron and antioxidants, sprinkle some on your salad, or try *halva*, a delicious confection of sesame seed paste and honey.

Sumac: Sumac is a spice made from the dried, powdered berries of a shrub that is common in the Middle East. Tangy in flavour, deep purple in colour, sumac grows in dense clusters. It is often sprinkled in salads like Fattoush (page 70) or used as a garnish.

✤ Tip: Toss some sumac into your kebab mix or marinades for a tangy twist.

Tahini: Essentially sesame paste, tahini is made by grinding raw or toasted sesame seeds.

✤ Tip: Tahini will separate from the natural sesame oil, stir to recombine and store upside down.

Vine leaves: These are the leaves of the grape vine. Green and slightly sour, most varieties are sold in a brine that you should rinse off the leaves before use.

✤ Tip: If you can find fresh vine leaves, use them to scoop up Tabbouleh (page 73) for a fantastic bite.

Za'atar: Dry oregano or thyme is often mixed with sumac, toasted sesame seeds and salt and served with olive oil and Arabic bread as a traditional breakfast in the Middle East.

✤ Tip: You can use za'atar to garnish Hummus (page 36) or labneh (yogurt spread), or toss into salad dressing.

BREAKFAST

BREAKFAST TRADITIONS

Some of my fondest memories of returning to Nazareth as an adult with my own family are of sitting around my parents' formidable breakfast table, recalling our morning traditions to my own children.

Each day began the same way: my mother roused her five stubborn children out of bed before she dashed off to her job as a school teacher. She didn't leave until she was positive we were *out of bed and standing up*. Though she didn't eat breakfast with us, she was as much a part of it as any of us. To this day, I marvel at the effortlessness with which she laid out an elaborate breakfast spread on busy weekdays. We were routinely treated to a dizzying array of jams and preserves, olives, honey, warm Arabic bread, olive oil, garden tomatoes, za'atar and labneh.

I can still taste the sunny flavour of my mother's homemade apricot jam, slathered on a chunk of toasted bread spread with a thin layer of sweet, creamy butter. The apricots came straight from the fruit trees in our backyard, as did the grapes and raspberries she used to boil with sugar and pectin to make the most delicious spreads. She prepared enough jams and fruit spreads to last until the trees bore fruit again the

following year. My dad broke open the apricot pits, removed the seeds and roasted them so they could be boiled with the jam, giving it an intense apricot flavour and a wonderful crunch.

Labneh, the tangy goats' milk yogurt cheese that can be found in every Middle Eastern pantry, was another staple on the breakfast table. My mother made several batches at a time, enough to last for a few months. She poured the goats' milk into a huge muslin-lined sieve, sea salted it, then let the whey drain overnight, or until it reached a consistency similar to farmers' cheese. She rolled the cheese into golf ball-sized orbs, dropped them in big jars and then filled them to the lip with the extra virgin olive oil her family harvested from their grove in the nearby village of El Rameh. In just a few days, the cheese was ready to eat.

And then there was za'atar. *Ahhhh*, za'atar. I so love this vibrant mix of wild thyme and oregano, lemony sumac and toasted sesame seeds that I ate it by the spoonful when I was pregnant with my children. In fact, I ate so much of it that my son, Tarek, can't stand to look at it, not to mention eat it! Regardless, on my family's breakfast table there always was

'WE WERE ROUTINELY TREATED TO A DIZZYING ARRAY OF JAMS AND PRESERVES, OLIVES, HONEY, WARM ARABIC BREAD, OLIVE OIL, GARDEN TOMATOES, ZA'ATAR AND LABNEH.'

– and still is and probably always will be – a dish of za'atar next to one of olive oil and a plate piled high with warm Arabic bread. There is perhaps no more delicious a way to start the day than tearing a piece of bread from the loaf, dunking it first in fruity olive oil, and then dipping it in za'atar mix. The exception being when my mother treated us to her homemade *manakeesh*, a flatbread topped with a mix of olive oil and za'atar and then baked.

Along with all of that, my mother always provided tomatoes cut in wedges and thinly sliced cucumbers – both picked from our garden, a big bowl of honey from my uncle's bee farm, chilli oil-cured green olives, and slices of halloumi (a semi-hard brined cheese made from either goats', sheep's or cows' milk) topped with fresh picked mint. The breakfast table fairly heaved with food! And although it may sound extravagant, the truth is,

such a feast is long on assembly, but short on preparation, requiring little, if any, actual cooking come breakfast time. Most of what we ate was either prepared months in advance or came straight from the garden. When it was time to go off to school, we simply covered the platters in cling film and put them in the cupboard or fridge until the next morning.

WEEKEND BREAKFASTS

Come the weekend, breakfasts were a bit more involved as they always included an egg dish or classic *foul* (a dip made from fava beans) in addition to the usual weekday repertoire. Since my mother worked on Saturdays, my father was the rare man who stepped into the kitchen to prepare his speciality egg dishes: Eggs and Potatoes (page 17) and Meat and Eggs (page 19). Such an arrangement was quite unusual back then – Middle Eastern men generally did not cook and women did not hold jobs on the weekend. These days, my husband, Wafa, has developed quite a reputation with our house guests for his Eggs with Za'atar (page 16). I make my own version of *Foul* (page 24), which is inspired by the classic (page 21), that my mother so lovingly prepared on Sunday, her only day off.

EGGS WITH ZA'ATAR

BAYID BI ZA'ATAR

Most households in the Levant place small dishes of olive oil and za'atar on the kitchen counter for snacking throughout the day. This recipe features eggs seasoned with those ingredients to create an excellent brunch dish. Whenever we have guests staying at our home in New York, which seems to be quite frequently (my son dubbed it the Hotel Bishara), my husband makes this fragrant meal, often cracking nearly a dozen eggs because one batch is never enough! To temper the assertive flavours of the za'atar and sumac, serve this with sliced tomatoes, cucumbers and some olives and a piece of feta, if you like.

In a small bowl, stir together the za'atar, sumac and salt and pepper; set aside.

Scoop out a penny-sized hole in the centre of each slice of bread.

Heat 60ml oil in a large frying pan over a medium heat. When hot, arrange half of the bread slices in the pan and brown for about 1 minute on each side. Reduce the heat to low and crack one egg into the hole in the middle of each slice of bread. Sprinkle the za'atar mixture over the egg, then cover and cook to your desired doneness, 2–3 minutes. If you like your yolk cooked really well, scoop up some oil from the bottom of the pan and drizzle over the top of each egg.

Using a spatula, transfer the toast with eggs to serving plates and keep warm. Repeat with the remaining oil and bread slices.

Serve warm with the tomatoes, cucumbers and feta cheese.

SERVES 6

3 tablespoons za'atar
1 tablespoon sumac
pinch of sea salt
½ teaspoon freshly ground black pepper
1 Italian country-style loaf, cut into
    5cm-thick slices (about 6 slices)
120ml extra virgin olive oil
6 medium eggs
sliced tomatoes, cucumbers and
    feta cheese, for serving

EGGS AND POTATOES

—— •◦• ——

BAYID WA BATATA

This dish brings back very fond memories of Saturday mornings at home with my father, who prepared this while my mother was at work. The funny thing is, he always closed the kitchen door for privacy while he cooked, but we were treated to quite a performance when my father ate. He did so quite ceremoniously, with lots of physicality, preparing each bite with the exact same ratio of Arabic bread to egg every time, then popping an olive and a slice of tomato into his mouth afterwards. You can add chopped fresh tomatoes and a finely diced pepper to the mix if you like; add them after sautéing the onions. Serve this dish straight from the pan with Arabic flatbread, sliced tomatoes and lemon wedges on the side.

⚜ **INGREDIENT NOTE** When cooking with chillies, I prefer using long green ones because they are milder than jalapeños, but if you like a bit more heat by all means use jalapeños. For an even milder flavour, use small green peppers instead.

Heat the oil in a medium frying pan and, when hot, sauté the onions until golden brown, about 2 minutes. Add the chilli, if using, and sauté until soft and fragrant, about 2 minutes, then tip in the potatoes and cook until they are browned and softened, 5–7 minutes.

Meanwhile, crack the eggs into a large bowl and whisk them together with the pepper, allspice and nutmeg, if using.

Pour the egg mixture into the potato mixture and stir constantly until the eggs are cooked to your desired consistency – 2–3 minutes for scrambled. Serve warm with Arabic bread, lemon wedges and sliced tomatoes.

SERVES 4–6

8 tablespoons extra virgin olive oil
1 small white onion, finely chopped
1 long green chilli, finely chopped (optional)
3–4 small Russet potatoes, peeled and cut into 1.2cm pieces
12 medium eggs
1½ teaspoons freshly ground black pepper
2 teaspoons ground allspice
⅓ teaspoon ground nutmeg (optional)
Arabic Bread (page 57), lemon wedges and sliced tomatoes, for serving

MEAT AND EGGS

—◦—

BAYID WA LAHMEH

My husband loves this breakfast of fluffy eggs and lamb seasoned with earthy spices, a classic my dad made on Saturday mornings. It makes a wonderful lunch or light dinner, too. Serve with a platter of olives, pickles, chillies, spring onions and radishes, all of which are refreshing to eat in-between bites of the creamy eggs. If you don't want to spend time chopping the lamb by hand, ask the butcher to put it through the mincer once only – you don't want the pieces to be too small.

Heat the oil in a large frying pan over a medium-high heat and sauté the shallots until soft and lightly browned, 3 minutes. Add the chilli and cook until soft, about 2 minutes, then stir in the allspice, salt, black pepper, nutmeg, cinnamon and cardamom, if using, and heat until fragrant, 30 seconds. Add the lamb and cook until it loses its pink colour, 4–5 minutes.

In a large bowl, whisk together the eggs, then pour them over the lamb mixture in the pan and leave to set. After a minute, stir occasionally until the eggs reach your desired consistency. Serve with the Arabic bread for scooping.

SERVES 4–6

60ml extra virgin olive oil or vegetable oil
1 shallot, cut into 6mm pieces
1 chilli, preferably jalapeño, deseeded, if desired, and finely chopped
½ teaspoon ground allspice
½ teaspoon sea salt
¼ teaspoon freshly ground black pepper
pinch of ground nutmeg
pinch of ground cinnamon
pinch of ground cardamom (optional)
500g lamb meat from the leg, chopped into 1.2cm pieces
10 medium eggs
Arabic Bread (page 57), for serving

SCRAMBLED EGGS WITH HALLOUMI

—◦—

BAYID WA HALLOUMI

Halloumi is a firm, salty, cheese made from a mix of goats' and sheep's milk. It's excellent for grilling or frying, as it holds together beautifully. Here it is cut into cubes and browned before the eggs are scrambled into it. The more frequently you make this dish, the more confident you will become at tinkering with the seasonings – or adding some new ones, like fresh coriander or basil.

Place a large frying pan over a high heat – don't choose a non-stick pan for this job. Add the oil and, when hot, fry the halloumi until golden on all sides, about 2 minutes in total. Stir in the tomato, salt, pepper and nutmeg and cook until the tomatoes have just softened, but are not falling apart.

Crack the eggs directly into the frying pan. After cracking the last egg, cook for 1 minute and then scramble the eggs with a fork, cooking for a further 2–3 minutes or longer, to achieve the texture you desire.

Serve warm with the Arabic bread and olives.

SERVES 6

60ml extra virgin olive oil
225–300g halloumi, cut into 2.5cm cubes
2 plum tomatoes, peeled and diced
1 teaspoon sea salt
½ teaspoon freshly ground black pepper
¼ teaspoon ground nutmeg
10–12 large eggs
Arabic Bread (page 57), plus black or green olives, for serving

SIMPLE OMELETTE

— ❖ —

IJII ARABIA

All of the ingredients for an Arab omelette are whisked together and cooked at once, unlike in its French counterpart, which rolls a filling into the centre of the cooked omelette. And while *ijii* literally translated means omelette, this egg dish more closely resembles a frittata: it is open-faced and the fillings are cooked right into the eggs. This is my mother's recipe, but there are endless variations.

SERVES 4–6

12 medium eggs
3 tablespoons chopped red or white onion
3 tablespoons chopped fresh
   flat-leaf parsley
1 tablespoon chopped fresh mint
pinch of sea salt, or to taste
pinch of ground nutmeg (optional)
1 chilli, finely chopped (optional)
60ml extra virgin olive oil

In a large bowl, combine the eggs, onion, parsley, mint, salt and nutmeg and chilli, if using, and whisk until the eggs are pale yellow.

Heat the oil in a frying pan over a medium-high heat and, when hot, pour in the egg mixture. Leave to cook, untouched, for 3 minutes, then lift up an edge of the omelette with an offset spatula to check the colour of the bottom. When it is golden brown, flip the omelette over and cook for a further 2 minutes.

Slide the omelette onto a large plate, cut into wedges and serve warm.

VARIATION *For a fancier version, my mother made six very thin individual omelettes. She whisked finely chopped plum tomatoes and a jalapeño into the egg mixture, then arranged cheese (depending on what she had to hand – Arabic, Cheddar, keshkaval, a yellow sheep's milk cheese that tastes somewhat like Cheddar, or goats' cheese) down the middle after she flipped it. To finish she folded the egg into thirds. Cook for 1 minute per side.*

BREAKFAST ON THE GO

My favourite weekday breakfast growing up was a sliced egg tucked inside warm bread, spread with labneh, topped with tomato slices and seasoned with a generous sprinkle of za'atar and pepper. *Kaak*, a delicious, chewy flatbread that's coated in sesame seeds and resembles an oversized bagel, was a close second. While it used to be baked at home, *kaak* is now widely available from the food carts that dot the streets of major Middle Eastern cities. Like the egg or cheese sandwich beloved in the West, it is the favoured breakfast for those on the go.

To prepare the sandwich, tear open the *kaak*, drizzle with a little olive oil and za'atar, then stuff with a sliced hard-boiled egg. I like to add a little chopped tomato and cucumber, too. The bread is available at Middle Eastern stores and some gourmet food stores. If you can't find *kaak*, use Arabic flatbread to make this nourishing portable breakfast.

FAVA BEAN BREAKFAST

— ·•· —

FOUL MUDAMMAS

Though this ancient dish is enjoyed all over the Middle East – particularly in the Levant – its roots lie in Egypt. *Foul* is a breakfast staple, but when I was growing up, it was a dish reserved for weekend eating, especially brunch. We would travel five hours to Jerusalem to walk the old market and eat *foul* at a diminutive place with just four tables – and a long queue outside. It was the place to eat it because the beans were prepared the traditional way – in clay pots set over a low fire and cooked for twelve hours. The table was also spread with boiled eggs, radishes, spring onions, chillies, pickled vegetables and, of course, hummus. It was set for lingering – and that's what we did, eating the best *foul* in the world while sipping coffee or tea. At Tanoreen, *foul* is a mainstay on our Sunday brunch menu – a big draw for those looking for a traditional Middle Eastern breakfast.

SERVES 4–6

400g dried fava beans, soaked and boiled
   (see right) or 2 (400g) tins, drained, a
   third of the liquid reserved, and rinsed
120ml extra virgin olive oil, plus extra
   for drizzling
120ml fresh lemon juice
4 garlic cloves, finely chopped
1 teaspoon sea salt
½ teaspoon ground cumin (optional)
2 tablespoons chopped fresh
   flat-leaf parsley

Combine the beans and 60ml oil in a large frying pan and bring to the boil over a medium heat. Remove from the heat and add the lemon juice, garlic, salt and cumin, if using, to the pan. Smash the bean mixture with a potato masher until the beans are just split or to the desired texture.

Spoon the *foul* into a serving bowl, smoothing the top with the back of a spoon and making a well in the centre. Drizzle the remaining olive oil into the well, garnish with parsley and serve. The *foul* will keep, covered, in the fridge for up to one week.

⚜ **COOKING TIP** My version of *foul* is slightly chunkier than most – I like to mash the beans only just until they split, but you can mash them smoother or to whatever consistency you desire. Serve it with *Tetbileh* (page 129) or Homemade Hot Sauce (page 194), or siracha (an Asian chilli sauce that you can source online), along with the traditional accompaniments mentioned above.

A GOOD SOAK

I always pre-soak dried beans at the restaurant, but I understand that it is not necessarily the most convenient technique for making bean dishes at home. That said, if you make extra large batches of beans and freeze some for later use, it's worth the effort as most of the cooking time isn't active. Here's my method:

Soak your desired amount of beans in a heavy-bottomed pot for 12 hours in enough water to cover by 10cm. Drain and return to the pot. Add enough water to cover by 10cm and add 1 tablespoon of salt for every 800g of beans. Cover, place over a high heat and bring to the boil. (If boiling dried chickpeas, add ½ teaspoon of bicarbonate of soda to speed up the cooking time.) Boil until you can crush a bean between your thumb and forefinger, 1–2 hours depending on the beans.

For a more intensely 'beany' flavour, simply bring the unsoaked beans, water and salt to the boil over a high heat, reduce the heat to low and cook for 4–5 hours. Drain, reserving the cooking water if boiling fava beans or chickpeas. To freeze, place the beans in 400g portions in resealable freezer bags and do the same with the fava bean or chickpea cooking water.

CHICKPEA AND FAVA BEAN BREAKFAST

MAKHLOOTA

Makhloota, literally translated, means 'mixture', which is precisely what this is. There are dozens of variations – some feature various kinds of beans, rice and bulgur – but my favourite is a traditional Palestinian version: chickpeas and favas seasoned with cumin, garlic and lemon juice. Serve this with Homemade Hot Sauce (page 194) or *Tetbileh* (page 129) and Arabic Bread (page 57), for scooping.

SERVES 4–6

300g dried fava beans, soaked and boiled (see page 21), 250ml cooking liquid reserved, or 2 (400g) tins fava beans, liquid from 1 tin reserved
200g dried chickpeas, soaked and boiled (see page 21) or 1 (400g) tin chickpeas, drained
180ml extra virgin olive oil
180ml fresh lemon juice
6 garlic cloves, finely chopped
1 tablespoon ground cumin, or to taste
1 teaspoon sea salt, or to taste
½ teaspoon freshly ground black pepper
1 jalapeño chilli, with seeds, cut into small dice for garnish
3 tablespoons chopped fresh flat-leaf parsley, for garnish
Arabic Bread (page 57), for serving

In a large frying pan, combine the favas and chickpeas with the reserved liquid. Set over a medium heat and bring to the boil. Reduce the heat to low and cook for 15 minutes, or until the liquid has almost completely evaporated. If the mixture goes dry before the beans are cooked, add a little water.

Pour in 60ml olive oil, reduce the heat and bring to a simmer, then cover and cook for 5 minutes. Add the lemon juice, garlic, cumin and salt, cover, turn off the heat and leave to sit for 2 minutes. Transfer to a serving bowl, drizzle over the remaining olive oil and garnish with the parsley and jalapeño. Serve with Arabic bread.

TANOREEN'S SPECIALITY FAVA BEANS

FOUL ALLA TANOREEN

The impulse to tinker with classics came to full bloom when I created this version of *foul* for Tanoreen. I integrated items typically served alongside traditional *foul* into the dish. The recipe calls for twice as many fava beans as you need. I did this as a favour to you; freeze them for next time.

SERVES 4–6

120ml extra virgin olive oil, plus extra for drizzling
800g dried fava beans, soaked and boiled (page 21) or 3 (400g) tins, drained and rinsed
3 shallots or 1 onion, diced
5 garlic cloves, finely chopped
1 mild green chilli, cored, deseeded and finely chopped
a big handful of chopped fresh coriander
3 plum tomatoes, diced
120ml fresh lemon juice
1 teaspoon ground cumin
1 teaspoon sea salt
1 teaspoon freshly ground black pepper (optional)
chopped fresh flat-leaf parsley, for garnish
Arabic Bread (page 57), for serving

In a large frying pan, combine 60ml oil with the beans and bring to the boil over a high heat. Meanwhile, in another large frying pan, heat the remaining 60ml oil over a medium heat until hot. Sauté the shallots or onion until golden brown and fragrant, about 3 minutes, then stir in the garlic until softened and fragrant, about 2 minutes. Add the chilli and cook until softened, and then the coriander, until darkened and wilted. Tip in the tomatoes and cook until they soften and release their juices, a further 3 minutes.

Add half the fava beans to the tomato mixture, along with the lemon juice, cumin, salt and pepper, if using, and mash the mixture until smooth. Transfer the *foul* to a serving bowl. Using the back of a spoon, make a moat in the centre and drizzle in a little olive oil. Garnish with parsley and serve with warm Arabic bread.

YOGURT TAHINI WITH CHICKPEAS

TISKAI

My Syrian friends shared this traditional breakfast with me when I first arrived in New York. It's been on the menu at Tanoreen since we opened our doors and is a favourite among my vegetarian customers. It's not a weekday breakfast dish, but rather a hearty brunch offering when paired with pickles, spring onions and radishes. I use low-fat yogurt because it's tangier than the full-fat version. You can toast the pine nuts in olive oil if you like, but they are traditionally toasted in ghee or butter for this dish.

In a large saucepan over a high heat, combine the chickpeas with the lemon juice, oil, garlic, cumin, salt and pepper. Bring to the boil, then immediately remove the pot from the heat; the chickpeas should be falling apart.

Heat a dash of oil, ghee or butter in a small frying pan over medium heat. Add the pine nuts and cook, stirring, until golden brown, about 2 minutes. Using a slotted spoon, transfer the nuts onto kitchen paper to drain.

In a medium bowl, combine the yogurt and tahini sauce. Using a wooden spoon or a hand mixer, beat until smooth. Transfer the mixture to a small frying pan and warm gently until just heated through – do not bring to the boil. Season to taste with lemon juice and salt if you need it.

To serve, arrange the toasted Arabic bread in the bottom of a serving dish. Spoon the chickpeas into the centre of the dish, nudging the pieces of bread to the edge of the dish. Spoon the warm yogurt mixture over the chickpeas. Garnish with the pine nuts and parsley and serve with chilli paste on the side.

SERVES 6–8

400g dried chickpeas, soaked (page 21)
    and boiled or 3 (400g) cans, drained
    and rinsed
120ml fresh lemon juice, plus extra
    for seasoning
60ml extra virgin olive oil or ghee or
    butter, plus extra for frying the nuts
5 garlic cloves, finely chopped, or to taste
1½ teaspoons ground cumin
1 tablespoon sea salt
¼ teaspoon freshly ground black pepper
60g pine nuts
250ml natural low-fat yogurt
120ml Thick Tahini Sauce (page 195;
    omit the parsley)
2 pieces Arabic Bread (page 57), cut into
    2.5cm squares, fried or toasted
3 tablespoons chopped fresh
    flat-leaf parsley
1 tablespoon seedless Middle Eastern or
    Turkish chilli paste (optional), to serve

HUMMUS WITH MEAT

— ◆ ◆ ◆ —

HUMMUS BIL LAHMEH

A heartier version of hummus, this features tender lamb seasoned with allspice and nutmeg that is then topped with toasted pine nuts and almonds. It's a wonderful brunch dish, but is just as appropriate for lunch or as a mezze. Be sure to use a tender cut of meat, because it is so quickly cooked. I always use more olive oil than butter, but you can swap the proportions if you like. Serve this with a small platter of Arabic Bread (page 57) spring onions, onions, hot chillies, olives, Pickled Turnips and Beetroot (page 188) and radishes.

Spread the hummus onto a shallow platter and make a well in the middle. Set aside.

Heat the oil and ghee or butter in a small frying pan over a medium heat and fry the almonds, stirring, for 1 minute. Add the pine nuts and cook, stirring, for a further 2 minutes until golden brown. Remove the nuts with a slotted spoon and transfer to paper towels.

Add the lamb, allspice, pepper, salt and nutmeg to the frying pan and sauté until medium to well done, 3–5 minutes. Return the nuts to the pan, stir to combine and cook for 30 seconds. Remove from the heat. Spoon the meat into the well of hummus on the plate and serve with fresh or toasted Arabic bread.

SERVES 4–6

400g Hummus (page 36)
3 tablespoons extra virgin olive oil
1 tablespoon ghee or butter
2 tablespoons slivered almonds, toasted
2 tablespoons pine nuts, toasted
250g lamb from the leg, cut into
   1.2cm pieces
½ teaspoon ground allspice
¼ teaspoon freshly ground black pepper
pinch of sea salt
pinch of ground nutmeg
Arabic Bread (page 57), fresh or toasted,
   for serving

MEZZE

EAT, TALK AND DRINK

The Italians have antipasti, the Spanish tapas, the Americans appetisers, the Chinese dim sum. In the Middle East, there is mezze, small plates of food served all at once to provide a bounty of tastes and textures. That said, one or two plates can comprise a snack, while a few more can add up to a whole meal. Mezze is invariably served with arak, an anise-flavoured spirit, to sip in between swipes of creamy dip on Arabic bread, forkfuls of fried or raw *kibbeh* and bites of spicy meat pies.

The simplest mezze are made up of whatever is to hand in the garden and the storecupboard. When I was growing up, this meant *makdous*, labneh, olives, hummus, Arabic bread, cucumbers and tomatoes.

At its core, though, mezze is a mood. In Arabic, the verb for mezze is *mezmiz*, which loosely translated means 'eat, talk and drink' – all at once. Imagine friends and family sitting around a table, passing heaped plates of hummus, baba ghanouj, falafel and za'atar bread, and laughing, talking – and of course debating heatedly – amid the clang of glasses and plates. Mezze is a ritual about sharing – not just bites of delicious food, but stories, experiences, laughter and opinions.

There are no real rules when it comes to serving mezze; several small plates and good company are the keys! When I visit one of my friends to play cards, she offers Hummus (page 36), romaine lettuce cups for scooping Tabbouleh (page 73) and a bowl of roasted nuts served with chilled glasses of *arak* or cold beer. When my children entertain guests, they serve *Mhammara* (page 42), toasted Arabic Bread (page 57) and some cheese with honey and crisp crackers. It can be that simple.

Admittedly, I tend towards the extravagant with my own mezze spreads, both at home and at Tanoreen. It is part of my culture to offer food in abundance and it begins with these small treasures. There are plenty of inspiring options to choose from in this chapter as well as in the salad chapter that follows. From among all of these recipes, you can create an array of dishes that beautifully capture the flavours and spirit of the Middle Eastern mezze table. The trick is not to overindulge if a main course follows; in fact, I often advise customers against ordering too much for fear they will be sated before the main course arrives!

The mezze dishes in this chapter easily cross over to other mealtimes – hummus is a favourite breakfast for many and an essential part of a wedding or cocktail party spread. Falafel (page 52), is a mezze staple, of course, but also makes an excellent lunch, tucked into Arabic bread and dressed with Thick Tahini Sauce (page 195).

But, always remember, to *mezmiz* is not so much dependent on the selection of dishes you provide at the table, as it is about the atmosphere you create around it. So, eat, talk, drink – and enjoy!

'ADMITTEDLY, I TEND TOWARDS THE EXTRAVAGANT WITH MY OWN MEZZE SPREADS, BOTH AT HOME AND AT TANOREEN. IT IS PART OF MY CULTURE TO OFFER FOOD IN ABUNDANCE AND IT BEGINS WITH THESE SMALL TREASURES.'

HOSSI FOR KIBBEH

— ⬧ —

KIBBEHH BIL HOSSI

I will never forget my mother making kibbeh this way. She would shape the meat mixture into small cones and then make the impression of a cross on them with the side of her hand. Along with a bottle of arak (it isn't proper to bring just a glass – the bottle is always on the table so that guests can have as much as they like) that always accompanied kibbeh, she put a bowl of *hossi*, a chilli paste fragrant with marjoram and cumin, in the centre of the table, then served one cone per plate. We flattened the kibbeh with the back of our forks, then spooned the *hossi* over it. There was always *saj*, a paper-thin bread, and a bowl of bright green olive oil. We dipped the bread in the olive oil, then used it to scoop up the kibbeh and *hossi*.

Heat 120ml of the oil in a frying pan over a medium-high heat. Add the onions and cook for about 15 seconds without stirring to prevent them from releasing their liquid. Continue cooking for 8–10 minutes in total, stirring only occasionally until the onions begin to caramelise. Using a slotted spoon, transfer the onions to a bowl.

Using the same frying pan, stir together the allspice, salt, cumin, pepper, marjoram and nutmeg until fragrant, about 10 seconds. Add the meat and sear on all sides, about 2 minutes in total, then reduce the heat and sauté for a further 3 minutes. Return the onions to the pan and cook for a further 3–5 minutes. Remove from the heat and stir in the chilli paste, if using. Add the almonds, pine nuts and walnuts, and mix together well. Divide the *hossi* into small bowls, one for each plate of kibbeh, and drizzle over the remaining olive oil.

Remove the kibbeh from the fridge and, with very clean hands, shape about 250g of the kibbeh mixture into a 12.5 x 5cm log. Using the side of your hand, make the impression of a cross in the top of each log. Repeat with remaining kibbeh to create 4–6 logs in total. Serve 1 log per plate and invite diners to spoon the *hossi* over the kibbeh.

SERVES 4–6

For the *Hossi*

250ml extra virgin olive oil, plus extra for dipping

2–3 large white onions, chopped

1 tablespoon ground allspice

1 teaspoon sea salt

⅔ teaspoon ground cumin

½ teaspoon freshly ground black pepper

¼ teaspoon dried marjoram

¼ teaspoon ground nutmeg

1kg lamb meat from the leg or lean beef, chopped

1–2 tablespoons seedless Middle Eastern or Turkish chilli paste (optional)

150g slivered almonds, toasted

75g pine nuts, toasted

75g walnuts, toasted (optional)

Kibbeh (page 35), chilled

KIBBEH: THE SOUND OF ONE VILLAGE POUNDING

An ominous title, but quite accurate. Galilean food traditions are many, but perhaps none is more significant than the preparation of kibbeh, a paste made from the freshest, leanest part of the goat or lamb mixed with fine bulgur wheat and regional spices. Traditionally, its presence on the table meant only one thing: there was something major to celebrate. It was otherwise too labour intensive, not to mention costly, to prepare for everyday eating. The only large gatherings that took place without kibbeh, in fact, were those veiled in sadness, such as the passing of a loved one.

Kibbeh is always made on the morning of the celebration. In the old days, every home had a huge stone pestle and mortar, typically stored out on the veranda, reserved for making this very special dish. The fresh meat was pounded with a pestle twice the width of a baseball bat that turned the ground meat into a paste-like dough. It's a tradition that continues to this day. I can still hear the booming of those pestles hitting the meat; the sound filled the air of my village, from house to house and street to street. It was welcome background music that left everyone in anticipation for a taste of this beloved dish.

I love all versions of kibbeh, but scooping it – raw – onto Arabic bread, then topping it with *Hossi* (page 32), a seasoned chilli paste, is a Proustian experience for me. It takes me straight back to those weekend mornings in the pretty village, Tarshiha, where I spent so much of my childhood. Today, kibbeh remains one of the most popular dishes in the Middle East. My father used to tell us there were over one hundred versions of kibbeh prepared in Aleppo, Syria, alone. When I moved to the States, where I made many Syrian friends, they confirmed this astonishing fact.

The basic and most traditional version of kibbeh is a dough made from the freshest minced goat meat kneaded together with bulgur wheat and spices. At my restaurant, I replace the goat with lamb and the consistency remains the same. Whichever meat you use, just remember: it must be extremely fresh, so purchase it only from a butcher you trust. There is nothing quite like raw kibbeh spread thinly on a plate, drizzled with fruity olive oil and chilli paste and topped with fresh mint and onion. It is the Middle Eastern version of steak tartare. The day after it is eaten raw, the kibbeh dough is traditionally layered in a tray with *hossi* then baked, or the kibbeh dough can be shaped into a cone filled with the *hossi* then deep-fried.

Cooked versions of kibbeh can be prepared from a dough made with ground fish (snapper, tilapia or tuna) accompanied by a *hossi* made from the same fish that's been chopped together with roasted pine nuts. I even make a vegan version of kibbeh at Tanoreen using ground pumpkin (mixed with spiced bulgur wheat) instead of meat. It's filled with a stuffing of fresh spinach and roasted walnuts bound together by pomegranate molasses.

RAW KIBBEH

No matter the preparation method – raw or cooked, hot or cold, shaped into balls or patties, spread onto a tray, baked, grilled, boiled or frozen – only the freshest, top-quality meat is acceptable for making kibbeh. In Nazareth, raw kibbeh was typically prepared on Saturday because that was always the day when meat was slaughtered and sold. The most tender, lean cuts of lamb or goat make the best kibbeh, but these days many people make it with beef because it's less expensive. As opposed to a good steak for grilling, the perfect meat for kibbeh has no fat and shows no marbling. In fact, I remember my mother drawing a fork through the meat after chopping it to remove any fatty strands or tendons. Here, kibbeh is served the Lebanese way, with mint and onions.

⚜ **COOKING TIPS** As with almost all Middle Eastern dishes, there are as many ways to spice kibbeh as there are cooks. In general, Palestinians like an assertively spiced kibbeh and serve it with hot sauce, while the Lebanese season it with a light hand.

When making kibbeh, make sure everything it touches – your hands, the bowls, the tray – is ice cold. Soak the bulgur wheat well; if you don't, it will take on excess water as you knead the dough.

Fill a small bowl with iced water. In a large bowl, combine the allspice, cumin, pepper, marjoram and nutmeg and stir in half the bulgur wheat. Dip your hands in the iced water and allow them to drip into the bulgur mixture, then press handfuls of the mixture between your palms to incorporate the spices, pressing and pushing it away from you as if kneading bread. Continue dipping your hands and dripping iced water into the bowl until you can squeeze a handful of the bulgur mixture in your hand and it stays together.

Add the remaining half of the bulgur wheat, the salt, chilli paste, white onion and minced meat and knead to incorporate as described above, until it forms a dough. (You will need about 120ml water in total to moisten the bulgur wheat and meat.)

If you plan to serve the kibbeh immediately, prepare an ice-water bath in an extra-large bowl and set the bowl of kibbeh in the ice water. If not serving right away, cover the kibbeh tightly with cling film and refrigerate for up to 1 hour while you prepare accompaniments, such as *hossi*. If there are leftovers, freeze in resealable plastic bags to bake or fry for up to 2 months. Press it into a tray or shape into balls before freezing. Frozen kibbeh is never served raw again.

To serve, spread 75g raw kibbeh on a small oval plate. Garnish with the mint leaves and onion slices and drizzle with olive oil.

SERVES 4–6

1 teaspoon ground allspice

½ teaspoon ground cumin, or to taste

½ teaspoon freshly ground black pepper

¼ teaspoon dried marjoram

¼ teaspoon ground nutmeg

200g fine bulgur wheat (#4), soaked in cold water for 30 minutes

1 teaspoon sea salt

1 tablespoon seedless Middle Eastern or Turkish chilli paste

½ white onion, grated or finely chopped in a food processor and drained on kitchen paper

500g very lean lamb or goat meat from the leg, minced to a paste

Hossi (page 32), for serving

fresh mint leaves and sliced white onion, for garnish

good-quality olive oil, for drizzling

HUMMUS

Hummus is perhaps the single most recognisable Middle Eastern dish in the world. It is essential on the mezze table, but it also serves as the base for Hummus with Meat (page 27) and the chickpea half of Chickpeas and Fava Beans (page 24). I serve hummus more than any other dish at Tanoreen; it is one of the items on our menu that has distinguished us from other Middle Eastern restaurants in the city.

How, you might wonder, can a combination of chickpeas, tahini, lemon juice and garlic vary so much from one kitchen to the next? The secret – apart from being fearless with the lemon juice and garlic – is in the cooking of the chickpeas. You must boil dried chickpeas until they not only lose their skins but are easily crushed between your thumb and forefinger. The boiling time can vary greatly depending on the quality of the chickpeas. I always boil far more chickpeas than I need, drain the excess and freeze them in resealable plastic bags for up to six months.

In a small bowl, place 50g of chickpeas and set aside for garnish.

In the bowl of a food processor, combine the remaining chickpeas, tahini, lemon juice, reserved liquid, garlic and salt. Process until smooth and creamy, adding more water or lemon juice to reach the desired consistency. (If you plan to refrigerate the hummus before serving, make it a little looser; it thickens up when chilled.) Taste and adjust the lemon juice and salt.

Transfer to a serving dish and, using the back of a spoon, make a well around the circumference of the dip, about 1.2cm from the edge. Drizzle the oil into the well and garnish with the reserved chickpeas and parsley. Serve with Arabic bread.

SERVES 6–8

500g dried chickpeas, soaked (page 21)
    and boiled, 250ml cooking liquid
    reserved, or 2 (400g) tins, liquid from
    1 tin reserved
300g tahini (sesame paste)
370ml fresh lemon juice, or to taste
5 garlic cloves or to taste, finely chopped
1 teaspoon sea salt
60ml extra virgin olive oil
2 tablespoons chopped fresh flat-leaf
    parsley, for garnish
Arabic Bread (page 57), for serving

MY MOTHER'S HUMMUS

HUMMUS BELZEIT

Whenever a dish called for tahini, my mother tried leaving it out because she felt that omitting it instantly lightened the dish. One of her most successful alterations was this version of hummus – prepared without tahini and with extra lemon juice – resulting in a much tarter spread. She also mashed the chickpeas by hand and left the mixture somewhat chunky. It is especially wonderful served warm with *Tetbileh* (page 129) drizzled over it. Serve this not only on the mezze table but also for breakfast with warm Arabic Bread (page 57), on sandwiches for lunch and as a spread with grilled meats for dinner.

In a large pot, combine the cooked chickpeas with the reserved liquid. Place over a low heat, bring to a gentle boil and, using a potato masher, crush the chickpeas until they are coarsely mashed. Remove from the heat.

With a wooden spoon, stir in 60ml oil, the lemon juice, garlic, chilli paste, if using, cumin and salt. Using the potato masher, mash again to incorporate all the ingredients. If the hummus is too stiff, gradually add a bit of bottled water (never tap) until it reaches the desired consistency. Taste and adjust the lemon juice, chilli paste and salt.

To serve, spread the hummus in a shallow bowl, drizzle with the remaining oil and garnish with parsley.

SERVES 8–10

500g dried chickpeas, soaked (page 21) and boiled, 250ml liquid reserved, or 2 (400g) tins, liquid from 1 tin reserved
120ml olive oil
180-250ml freshly squeezed lemon juice
6 garlic cloves or to taste, finely chopped
1 teaspoon seedless Middle Eastern or Turkish chilli paste (optional)
1 teaspoon ground cumin, plus extra to taste
1 teaspoon sea salt, or to taste
2 tablespoons chopped fresh flat-leaf parsley, for garnish

TAHINI WITH PARSLEY SAUCE

BAKDONSIYYEY

This versatile sauce, known perhaps more widely by its Lebanese name, *taratour*, is both a dip and a sauce on the mezze table. Swab it onto a small folded piece of Arabic bread in between sips of arak, or drizzle it over falafel to give the chickpea patties a lemony kick. *Bakdonsiyyey* is always served alongside Whole Fried Fish (page 129), and is sometimes converted into a salad to accompany the fish by adding chopped fresh tomatoes and cucumbers.

In a small bowl, mix together the tahini sauce, parsley and lemon zest. If you prefer a thinner sauce, add the lemon juice or 2 tablespoons water. Stir in the jalapeño for a spicy kick, if desired. The sauce will keep, tightly covered in the fridge, for a few days if the parsley is incorporated, or for up to 1 week if the parsley is added as you serve it.

MAKES 375ML

250ml Thick Tahini Sauce (page 195)
60g chopped fresh flat-leaf parsley
zest of ½ lemon
juice of ½ lemon or 2 tablespoons water (optional)
½ jalapeño chilli, grated (optional)

AUBERGINE PÂTÉ

—— ◦•◦ ——

I came up with this recipe when I discovered the very large, deep purple aubergines in American markets. The idea that I could slice an aubergine into 20cm-wide rounds was revelatory! So, rather than char them and scoop out the flesh, I decided to slice and fry (or roast) these jumbo aubergines, then use them as a base for a salad. This recipe calls for a lot of lemon juice, but keep in mind that the aubergine soaks up sauce like a sponge. For this dish, I prefer to peel tomatoes, but it is not absolutely necessary. In addition to making a creative mezze, these salad-topped rounds make a great vegan sandwich: just tuck one into Arabic Bread (page 57) or serve alongside falafel.

Arrange the aubergine slices on a baking sheet, sprinkle with salt and set aside for 30 minutes or until the aubergine begins to sweat. Pat dry.

Add 6mm vegetable oil to a large frying pan and place over a high heat. When hot and working in batches, use a spatula to slide the aubergine slices into the frying pan and fry, turning once, until they are medium brown on both sides, about 4 minutes in total. Repeat with the remaining aubergine, adding more oil to the pan if necessary. Alternatively, brush the aubergine slices with oil on both sides and roast in a 250°C/gas mark 9 oven until golden, turning once, about 15 minutes in total. Set aside to cool.

Meanwhile, in a medium bowl, combine the tomatoes, chopped chillies, garlic, 120ml olive oil, lemon juice, salt and pepper. Stir well to incorporate and gradually add as much of the remaining olive oil as necessary to achieve your desired consistency. Spoon enough of the tomato mixture onto each aubergine slice to leave a narrow border around the rim. Garnish with the sliced chillies and serve.

SERVES 8

3 medium aubergines (1.25–1.5kg),
    cut into 1.2cm rounds
sea salt, for sprinkling
vegetable oil, for frying
80–120ml extra virgin olive oil, for tomato
    topping, plus extra for sautéing
    or roasting
4 long green or jalapeño chillies,
    2 deseeded (optional) and diced,
    2 finely sliced
8 plum tomatoes or 3 beefsteak tomatoes,
    peeled and diced
6 garlic cloves, crushed
juice of 2 lemons
freshly ground black pepper

BABA GHANOUJ

—◆—

Every country in the Levantine region claims this earthy, robust spread as its own and, in truth, it might simply be because there are many ways to season *baba ghanouj*. On the West Bank and in Gaza, most cooks use red tahini made from sesame seeds that are roasted for a longer time than the white seeds. Many cooks also use pomegranate molasses instead of lemon juice. Some garnish with parsley, others with pistachios, and still others with pomegranate seeds. And it goes on and on.

My version is rather straightforward, intensely smoky and a touch more tart than most. In Nazareth, we call this spread *mutabal* (I had never heard it called baba ghanouj until I came to New York), a name used in other parts of the Middle East for an entirely different aubergine spread made without tahini (for that recipe, see opposite).

⚶ COOKING TIP My dad used to say that the key to making excellent baba is to begin with grilled aubergine made by setting the vegetable directly over hot coals or the flame of a gas stove, imparting a lovely smoky flavour. But if you want a milder flavour, roast the aubergines in the oven; directions are provided for both methods below. You can use any kind of aubergine you like, but ideally choose a variety with few seeds and avoid especially large aubergines, as they taste bitter. I prefer the black Italian aubergine; I find it has the fewest seeds.

Prepare a charcoal or gas grill for grilling over a high heat, or turn a gas burner to high. Place the aubergines directly onto the coals or, one at a time, on the flame and grill, using tongs to turn the vegetables as the skin chars, until blackened all over. Set aside to cool.

Alternatively, to roast the aubergines, preheat the oven to 250°C/gas mark 9 and line a baking sheet with aluminium foil. Pierce the aubergines in a few places with a sharp knife, then place them on the prepared baking sheet and roast, turning every 5 minutes or so, until the skin is blistered and begins to crack all over. Set aside to cool.

Slice the aubergines in half lengthways and scoop out the flesh, transferring it directly to a colander to allow the liquid to drain.

Transfer the drained aubergine to a medium bowl. Add the tahini sauce to the aubergine and mash them together with a fork, breaking up the larger pieces of aubergine with a knife, if necessary. Stir in the garlic along with lemon juice to taste. Spoon the baba ghanouj into a shallow serving dish and, using the back of a spoon, make a well around the circumference of the dip, about 1.2cm from the edge. Drizzle oil into the well, garnish with parsley and serve with Arabic bread.

SERVES 6–8

3 medium aubergines (1.25–1.5kg)
370ml Thick Tahini Sauce (page 195)
2 garlic cloves, crushed
fresh lemon juice or pomegranate
    molasses, to taste
60ml extra virgin olive oil
2 tablespoons chopped fresh flat-leaf
    parsley, for garnish
Arabic Bread (page 57), for serving

MUTABAL

In most Middle Eastern countries (apart from Nazareth, where baba ghanouj is called *mutabal*), the ingredients in this dish are as simple as aubergine, garlic and lemon juice – a lightened up, tahini-free version of baba ghanouj. But when I arrived in America, I experimented with various ingredients and found myself adding tomatoes, chilli and a hint of cumin to my *mutabal*. I serve it with grilled meat and chicken. My children love this preparation, which is also great spread on toasted or fresh Arabic bread, crusty flatbread or crackers.

Prepare a charcoal or gas grill for grilling over a high heat, or turn 3 gas burners to high. Place the aubergines directly onto the coals or flame and grill, using tongs to turn them as the skin chars, until blackened all over. Set aside to cool.

Alternatively, roast the aubergine in the oven. Preheat the oven to 200°C/gas mark 6 and line a baking sheet with aluminium foil. Pierce the aubergines in a few places with a sharp knife, place them on the prepared baking sheet and roast, turning every 5 minutes or so, until the skin is blistered and begins to crack all over. Set aside to cool.

Slice the aubergines in half lengthways and scoop out the flesh, transferring it directly to a colander to allow the liquid to drain.

Meanwhile, in a medium bowl, combine the tomatoes with the chillies, if using, garlic, shallot, half the parsley, 3 tablespoons oil, lemon juice, cumin, pepper and salt. Add the drained aubergine and mix together with a fork. Transfer the aubergine mixture to a serving bowl and drizzle with the remaining 3 tablespoons oil. Garnish with the remaining parsley and surround with the cucumber slices.

SERVES 6–8

3 medium aubergines (1.25–1.5kg)
4 plum tomatoes, finely chopped
2 chillies, deseeded and finely chopped
   (optional)
4–5 garlic cloves, crushed
1 shallot, very finely chopped
60g chopped fresh flat-leaf parsley
6 tablespoons extra virgin olive oil,
   or to taste
juice of 2 lemons, plus extra for finishing
½ teaspoon ground cumin, or to taste
½ teaspoon freshly ground black pepper
sea salt, to taste
sliced cucumbers, for garnish

RED PEPPER AND WALNUT SPREAD

—— ◆ ——

MHAMMARA

This very popular walnut and red pepper spread, similar to Spain's *romesco*, is both piquant and sweet. Some trace the dish's origins to Aleppo, Syria, while the Turks claim it as their own. I learned to make this version from Syrian friends I met in my early days in New York. Of course, I couldn't help fiddling with the recipe – mine is full of walnuts and homemade breadcrumbs to replace the traditional cracked wheat. I also strain it of most of its moisture. *Mhammara* is traditionally served with toasted Arabic bread, but it also makes an excellent addition to a crudité platter. Because the richness and texture of the walnuts lends a meatiness to this dish, I often suggest it as a vegetarian substitute for raw Kibbeh (page 35).

Combine the peppers and onion in the bowl of a food processor and purée until smooth. Line a colander with kitchen paper and transfer the mixture to the colander; allow it to drain for at least 30 minutes. Transfer the pepper mixture to a medium bowl and set aside.

Place the walnuts in the bowl of the food processor and pulse until just coarsely chopped; do not process to a paste. Alternatively, chop with a knife. Set aside 2 tablespoons for garnish.

Add the rest of the walnuts, the breadcrumbs, 2 tablespoons pomegranate molasses, oil, cumin, allspice, nutmeg, chilli paste, salt and pepper to the pepper mixture and stir until thoroughly combined. Cover and refrigerate for 30 minutes or until cool.

Transfer the mixture to a serving dish, drizzle with the remaining pomegranate molasses and garnish with the reserved chopped and whole walnuts. Serve at room temperature.

SERVES 6–8

4 large or 6 small red peppers, 750g–1kg in total, deseeded and chopped
1 small white onion, chopped
300g chopped walnuts plus a few whole walnuts, for garnish
60g fresh breadcrumbs
80ml pomegranate molasses
6 tablespoons extra virgin olive oil
1½ teaspoons ground cumin seeds
½ teaspoon ground allspice
¼ teaspoon freshly grated nutmeg
2 tablespoons seedless Middle Eastern or Turkish chilli paste or to taste (optional)
sea salt and freshly ground black pepper

BRUSSELS SPROUTS WITH PANKO

Brussels sprouts were not part of the Palestinian kitchen when I was growing up. I discovered them here in the States and very eagerly tried to push them on my children. To that end, I did what any good mother would do – I pumped up their flavour by adding a little tahini sauce and pomegranate molasses. It worked! In fact these Brussels sprouts made it onto the original Tanoreen menu and I've never taken them off. Not long ago, I emerged from the kitchen to a round of applause from a table of twelve, none of whom liked Brussels sprouts until I convinced them to try these. It's become one of the restaurant's most popular dishes.

Pour 6–12mm vegetable oil in a large frying pan and place over a high heat. When hot, to test the temperature, slip half a Brussels sprout into the pan; if it makes a popping sound, the oil is hot enough. Working in batches, fry the Brussels sprouts, turning occasionally, until they are browned all over, 2–3 minutes. Using a slotted spoon, transfer the sprouts to a kitchen-paper-lined plate to drain.

Meanwhile, whisk together the tahini sauce, yogurt and pomegranate molasses in a medium bowl. Set aside.

In a small frying pan, heat the olive oil over a medium-high heat. When hot, sauté the garlic until fragrant, about 1 minute. Add the panko and stir constantly until the crumbs are golden brown, about 2 minutes. Sprinkle in the salt and remove the breadcrumbs from the heat. Transfer to a paper-towel–lined plate to cool. Place the Brussels sprouts in a serving dish, drizzle with the sauce and top with the panko crumbs. Serve immediately.

SERVES 6–8

vegetable oil, for frying
2kg Brussels sprouts, outer leaves removed, cut in half
250ml Thick Tahini Sauce (page 195)
250ml plain yogurt
2 tablespoons pomegranate molasses
2 tablespoons extra virgin olive oil
½ teaspoon finely chopped garlic
100g panko (Japanese-style breadcrumbs)
pinch of sea salt

TURKISH SALAD

SALATA TURKIYYA

This dish causes some confusion among my customers who expect a tomato salad, which is what most New York restaurants consider a Turkish salad. In Nazareth, the vegetables are chopped very finely and tossed with hot sauce thickened with tomato paste. Typically one of a trio of spreads on the mezze table, along with Hummus (page 36) and Baba Ghanouj (page 40), this is also great on Falafel (page 52) or with Chicken Kebabs (page 146).

COOKING TIP If making ahead, add the cucumber just before serving; without it, this salad, topped with a little olive oil, keeps in the fridge for up to 10 days.

In a large bowl, combine the cucumbers and onions with the hot sauce, tomato purée, garlic, cumin, allspice, pepper, lemon juice and oil. Using a rubber spatula, gently stir until evenly distributed. Transfer to a serving dish, drizzle with olive oil and serve.

SERVES 8–10

2 Persian seedless cucumbers, peel on, finely diced
2 small red or white onions, finely diced
250ml Homemade Hot Sauce (page 194), or 150g harissa paste
4 tablespoons tomato purée
3–4 garlic cloves, finely chopped
1 teaspoon ground cumin, or to taste
1 teaspoon ground allspice
1 teaspoon freshly ground black pepper
juice of 2 lemons
120ml extra virgin olive oil, plus extra for drizzling

PICKLED STUFFED AUBERGINE

— ▪◆▪ —

MAKDOUS

Pickles of all sorts are a staple at every Middle Eastern meal. This particular pickle is generally served as part of an extensive mezze platter (although it makes a great hors d'oeuvres, too). It has a complex character and is more elaborate than most to prepare. I love the heat that the chilli paste contributes to the stuffing, but you can use a milder chilli or none at all. If sealed properly, *makdous* can last for months in your store cupboard.

✦ **INGREDIENT NOTE** Primarily a preservative, lemon salt speeds up the process of pickling so that you can eat the aubergine right away and I use it to avoid using lemon juice, which when mixed with the oil, will drain out of the aubergine.

Bring a large pot of salted water to the boil. Meanwhile, using a sharp kitchen knife, make two incisions anywhere on each aubergine to prevent them from floating in the water, taking care not to cut all the way through. Slide the aubergines into the boiling water and cook until tender, about 20 minutes, then transfer to a large colander to drain. Lay a piece of greaseproof paper directly onto the aubergines, and place heavy tins on top to compress them. Leave to sit for at least 4 hours or overnight to drain thoroughly.

In a medium bowl, combine the walnuts, garlic, oil, chilli paste, lemon salt and sea salt. Using a sharp kitchen knife, slit each aubergine lengthways from stem to root end, cutting through the slits made in the previous step. Divide the walnut mixture evenly among the aubergine halves. Layer the aubergines, stuffing-side up, in a sterilised glass container and pour over enough oil to cover them completely. Place a piece of greaseproof paper on top so that it is touching the aubergines. Seal tightly and leave to stand at room temperature for 5–7 days. To serve, arrange the *makdous* on a large plate, drizzle with olive oil and serve with warm Arabic bread.

MAKES 10–12 PICKLES

10–12 small Italian aubergines
450g chopped walnuts
10 garlic cloves, crushed
60ml extra virgin olive oil, plus extra for
   jarring and serving
2 heaped tablespoons seedless Middle
   Eastern or Turkish chilli paste (optional)
1 tablespoon lemon salt
2 tablespoons sea salt, plus extra to taste
Arabic Bread (page 57), for serving

VEGETARIAN VINE LEAVES

————— ·•· —————

WARAK ANAB BIL ZAIT

Stuffed vine leaves should be about the length and width of a woman's pinkie finger – far more slender than most of the versions I see in the States. The size of the vine leaves themselves can vary; if they are larger than 10cm across, cut them in half along the vein, beginning at the tip of the leaf. The stuffed leaves can be frozen in an airtight container for up to four months. To thaw, set them out on the counter or in the fridge overnight.

In a large bowl, combine the tomatoes and rice with the parsley, onions, oil, lemon juice, tomato purée, mint, allspice, 1 teaspoon salt, dried mint, pepper, nutmeg and cumin. Using a wooden spoon, stir the stuffing until all the ingredients are thoroughly mixed together.

Working with 1 vine leaf at a time, snip the stem off with kitchen shears. Lay the vine leaf on a clean work surface, shiny-side down with the stem end facing you. If the indentations in the leaf are deep, close them up by cutting them in half and overlapping the two segments or by patching the indentations with a piece of another leaf. Repeat with the rest of the leaves, stacking them as you go.

Arrange the carrot, potato or tomato slices on the bottom of a 3.75-litre stockpot (this prevents the vine leaves on the bottom layer from burning) and set aside.

Spoon 1 tablespoon of the stuffing onto the base of a leaf, just above the stem. Bring the bottom of the leaf up over the filling, then fold the sides of the leaf into the filling. Roll the leaf away from you, wrapping it as tightly as possible around the filling to keep it all in. Repeat with the remaining leaves and filling. As each leaf is rolled, place it in the prepared pot, arranging the stuffed vine leaves in concentric rings, beginning from the outside and working your way to the centre. Pack the rolls snugly side by side. When the bottom of the pot is covered, layer the remaining rolls on top.

Combine 500ml water with the remaining ½ teaspoon salt and add to the pot. Invert a small, heatproof plate directly on top of the vine leaves, then place the lid on the pot. Bring to the boil over a high heat, then reduce the heat to low and cook for 40 minutes–1 hour, until the rice is tender and the vine leaves are easily pierced with a fork.

To serve, remove the plate from the vine leaves, and using a fork, gently transfer the vine leaves to a serving plate and garnish with the vegetables. Alternatively, holding a tea towel, press the small plate against the rolls and tip the pot to drain off the liquid. Remove the plate. Invert a serving plate over the pot and flip the pot over to transfer the vine leaves and vegetables to the platter. Gently remove the pot. Serve with the lemon wedges.

MAKES 50–60 VINE LEAVES (SERVES 8–10)

6 plum tomatoes or 5 beefsteak tomatoes, chopped
300g Egyptian rice
90g chopped fresh flat-leaf parsley
2 medium white onions, chopped
120ml extra virgin olive oil
juice of 2 lemons, or to taste
1 tablespoon tomato purée
1 tablespoon chopped fresh mint
1 tablespoon ground allspice
1½ teaspoons sea salt, or extra to taste
1 teaspoon dried mint
1 teaspoon freshly ground black pepper
½ teaspoon ground nutmeg
½ teaspoon ground cumin
1 (450g) jar vine leaves, rinsed
carrots, potatoes or tomatoes, cut into 6mm-thick slices (enough to line the bottom of a 3.75-litre pot)
lemon wedges, for garnish

Picture opposite, clockwise from top right: za'atar bread, pickled stuffed aubergine, vegetarian grape leaves, labneh, marinated olives, baba ghanouj, tabouleh, pickled chillies and pickled cauliflower and carrots.

OF MARRIAGE AND MEZZE

Galileans love a celebration, but there is perhaps none more ebullient than a wedding. And there was perhaps no better example from my youth than the marriage of my uncle Elia and aunt Marie. I was just seven years old and it was unlike any other gathering I had been to – it has become a defining memory of my childhood. I can still recall every whiff of aromatic spice and the gloriously vibrant platters of food as if I were there mere minutes ago.

A festive feeling filled the air long before the day of the actual wedding ceremony. Traditionally, the groom's parents host nightly get-togethers for his family and friends throughout the week leading up to the wedding day. Mezze is served every night.

During the day, the women in the family gathered and prepared vast amounts of food for the guests – fresh baked spinach pies, grassy chopped flat-leaf parsley, tomatoes and cucumbers picked fresh from their own gardens and chopped finely for tabouleh. Each night just before the feasts, the women made raw kibbeh so it was supremely fresh. It was an enormous amount of work, but Palestinians take pride in

making every dish from scratch. Such a convivial spirit is as much a part of mezze as the spread of dishes itself.

A few days before the wedding, uncle Elia drove from Tarshiha to collect my family in Nazareth. My brothers and sisters and I piled into the back of his covered pick-up truck, while he and my parents sat three across, up front. Off we went, on a windswept, hour-long ride through the Galilean countryside. There were groves of banana and avocado trees, field after field of cucumbers, every fig varietal imaginable and trees bursting with olives. We sang ourselves hoarse with repeated renditions of our English ABCs, a tune my teacher mother insisted we sing until we knew it inside out!

As we approached Tarshiha, a hillside village of five thousand where my father was born and we spent our summers, the singing slowed and our eyes grew increasingly wide. The lush village, about eight miles south of the Lebanese border, was overrun with emerald-green grape vines and citrus trees. The rooftops were quilted in trays of colourful fruits and vegetables set out to dry in the sun. Crimson tomatoes, earthy wheat berries, green okra, red peppers dried for mixing into

kibbeh, *mhlookia* leaves, black figs, tobacco leaves and purple aubergines strung along rope with garlic were all part of the bountiful harvest, preserved for the winter months.

After the ceremony my uncle and new aunt walked arm in arm behind a *sahje*, a greeting line of men that stretched and moved from the village church to their new home. This ancient tradition isn't as closely observed these days as it once was, but back then, the ritual lasted for nearly an hour.

Later in the evening, the *real* celebration began – in a friend's backyard that was converted into a reception space. There were rows of banquet tables draped in crisp white linens, each one set with several bottles of *arak*, the anise-flavoured aperitif that is the regional drink of the Levant, and most importantly ... mezze.

Every table was covered from end to end with dishes of velvety hummus, smoky mutabal, the fluffiest tabbouleh, crispy fried and raw kibbeh, labneh, mile-high piles of Arabic bread, and spinach and meat pies. (In the Middle Eastern culinary tradition, less is never more!) But as overwhelmed as I was by the abundance and joy of the occasion, it was the way

my mother took charge of the cooking on this and so many other occasions that left the biggest and most lasting impression on me. She managed to create a feeling of togetherness and a sense of family that is hard to replicate. From my uncle's wedding day on, I dreamed of being able to cook like my mother. And I still do.

'EVERY TABLE WAS COVERED FROM END TO END WITH DISHES OF VELVETY HUMMUS, SMOKY MUTABAL, THE FLUFFIEST TABBOULEH, CRISPY FRIED AND RAW KIBBEH, LABNEH, MILE-HIGH PILES OF ARABIC BREAD, AND SPINACH AND MEAT PIES.'

FALAFEL

—◆—

It is to Arabs what a hamburger is to Americans: falafel is Middle Eastern fast food. In Nazareth, falafel stands are on what seems like every street corner. You order, add your own salads and pickles, and eat quickly. But as ubiquitous as it is, falafel can vary wildly in proportion of seasonings from vendor to vendor and from country to country.

Unlike at home, where falafel is typically served with tahini sauce or hot sauce (see my homemade versions on pages 195 and 194), street falafel offers a smorgasbord of toppings and sauces that turns the humble patties into something extraordinary. I love mine stuffed into pitta and topped with fried aubergine, pickles, *Tetbileh* (page 129), fresh lemon juice, pickled purple aubergine, red cabbage salad and chopped tomatoes as well as various sauces.

⚜ **COOKING TIP** The beauty of the falafel mix is that you can use as much as you need and then refrigerate or freeze the rest. It always tastes best fresh, but if you have leftover mixture, place it in a resealable plastic bag, press all the air out and seal it. It will keep in the fridge for up to 6 days and in the freezer for 2 months.

Place the onion in the bowl of a food processor and process until very finely chopped. With the motor running, add the garlic through the feed tube and chop very finely, followed by the parsley, coriander and chilli. Stop the motor, add the chickpeas and process until you can squeeze a portion of the mixture in your palm and it comes together easily but isn't too 'pastey'.

Transfer the falafel mixture to a mixing bowl. Add the coriander, cumin, sea salt and bicarbonate of soda. Using your hands or a rubber spatula, gently incorporate the spices while tossing the mixture in the same way you would a salad. Set aside until ready to fry.

Fill a large, deep frying pan with 5cm oil. Place over a high heat until hot (185–190°C) or when a tiny piece of the mix, dropped into the hot oil, creates bubbles and floats to the surface. Have two large trays ready, one lined with kitchen paper.

Meanwhile, shape the falafel. Using a falafel moulder, known as an *aleb*, or with dampened hands, scoop up a walnut-size portion of the dough and roll it into a ball. Press the ball between your palms to make a 4–5cm-wide patty, taking care not to compress the dough or squeeze the moisture out of it. Place the patty on the unlined tray and continue shaping half the dough.

Once the oil is hot, begin frying. Using a slotted spoon or your hands, carefully slip the patties into the pot, working in batches. Do not crowd the pot. When the patties float to the surface, flip them over with the slotted spoon and cook until mahogany brown, about 5 minutes. Transfer to the kitchen-paper-lined tray to drain.

While the patties are frying and draining, shape the remaining dough into patties and fry as above. Serve hot with Arabic flatbread, tahini sauce and a selection of pickles.

SERVES 8

1 large white onion, quartered
6 garlic cloves, peeled
60g coarsely chopped fresh flat-leaf parsley
30g coarsely chopped fresh coriander
1 chilli, preferably jalapeño, deseeded if desired and coarsely chopped
1kg dried chickpeas, soaked
3 tablespoons ground coriander
2 tablespoons ground cumin
1 tablespoon sea salt
⅓ teaspoon bicarbonate of soda
vegetable oil, for frying
Arabic Bread (page 57), pickles and Thick Tahini Sauce (page 195), for serving

MEAT PIES

∙•∙

SFEEHA

Sfeeha is a very traditional Levantine snack and was one of my mother's favourite things to make when I was growing up. She would spend hours making the buttery dough, which turned out more like puff pastry than my version here.

Though often served slightly larger, I have sized these as starters – plate a few next to a salad or soup if you want a proper meal. Traditional *sfeeha* fillings are mainly variations on cheese, spinach or meat. But, by all means, mix and match any manner of seasoned vegetables, cheeses or meat toppings as you like.

Combine the yeast and sugar in a small bowl. Stir in 60ml warm water, then leave to stand until the yeast dissolves and the mixture becomes a thin paste.

Meanwhile, sift the flour into a large bowl. Sprinkle the flour with the mahlab and mastic, if using. Make a well in the centre of the bowl, sprinkle in the salt and tip in the yeast mixture, then add the remaining water. Pour the yogurt and oil into the well and, using your hands, begin incorporating the flour into the liquid from the outside edge to the inside edge until it all comes together. Alternatively, combine all the ingredients in the bowl of a freestanding mixer fitted with the dough hook and mix on medium speed until the dough comes together.

Turn the dough out onto a clean work surface and knead until it is smooth and pliable, 3–5 minutes. Divide the dough into 5 equal pieces, shape into balls and arrange on a baking sheet. Cover with a tea towel and set aside in a warm, draught-free place for 30 minutes.

Dust a clean work surface and a rolling pin with flour. Working with 1 ball at a time, roll out the dough into a 40cm round. Using a 7.5cm biscuit cutter, cut out the dough and transfer to a baking sheet, leaving 2.5cm between each one. Cover with a tea towel and let the dough rest in a warm, draught-free place for about 40 minutes. Using your fingertips, tap the rounds all over, leaving small indentations in the surface.

To make the pies: preheat the oven to 175°C/gas mark 4 and grease a baking sheet with the oil. Spoon 2 tablespoons filling into the centre of each dough round. For the spinach pies, bring the edges of the dough together in three flaps to form a triangle. Using the back of a spoon, press the filling into the creases of the pie. For the meat pies and cheese pies, leave open-faced or pinch the dough together on opposite sides of the disc to form a boat, pushing the meat into the creases with the back of a spoon. Bake until the dough is golden and the filling is warmed through, 12–15 minutes.

MAKES 8 X 20CM PIES OR 60 X 7.5CM PIES

1 tablespoon fast-acting dry yeast
1 tablespoon sugar
500ml warm water, plus extra if needed
500g flour (250g each wholewheat flour and plain flour) or 500g potato flour (for a gluten-free option)
1 teaspoon mahlab (optional)
pinch of mastic (optional)
1½ teaspoons sea salt, or to taste
125ml natural yogurt
60ml extra-virgin olive or vegetable oil, plus extra for greasing
Meat, Spinach or Cheese Fillings (pages 55–56)

⁂ **INGREDIENT NOTE** Although not essential, I like to use mahlab, a fragrant spice made from the ground kernels inside St Lucie cherry pits in this dough. It is generally used for sweet doughs, but I love the subtle hint of floral, nutty, vanilla-like flavour that it lends to this savoury dough. Mastic, the resin of the Greek *Pistacia lentiscus* tree, is another exotic flavouring that tinges the dough with a barely-there liquorice flavour.

MEAT PIE FILLING

SFEEHA BIL LAHMEH

MAKES ENOUGH FOR 8 X 20CM PIES OR 60 X 7.5CM PIES

120ml extra virgin olive oil
200g finely diced white onion
1 tablespoon ground allspice
½ teaspoon ground nutmeg
⅓ teaspoon ground cinnamon
½ teaspoon ground cumin
½ teaspoon sea salt or to taste
½ teaspoon freshly ground black pepper
pinch of ground cardamom (optional)
1.5kg lamb meat from the leg, chopped
370ml natural yogurt
120ml Thick Tahini Sauce (page 195)
1 tablespoon pomegranate molasses (optional)
juice of 1 lemon
75g pine nuts, toasted (optional)
150g slivered almonds, toasted

Heat the oil in a frying pan over a medium-high heat and sauté the onion until soft and fragrant, about 5 minutes. Add the allspice, nutmeg, cinnamon, cumin, salt, pepper, cardamom, if using, and lamb and cook just until the meat is thoroughly coated with the spices – do not overcook. Remove from the heat and stir in the yogurt, tahini sauce, pomegranate molasses, if using, lemon juice, pine nuts, if using, and almonds; and mix together well.

MASTIC MEMORIES

Whenever I open my jar of fragrant mastic, it takes me straight back to the church in Nazareth where my family and I attended Sunday services. Communion was not paper-thin wafers, but rather delicious chunks of bread baked with this aromatic sap of the mastic tree by the women from surrounding villages. They not only baked enough thick, tender loaves to serve in pieces, but provided every family with a loaf to take home. I suppose it is essentially nostalgia that inspires me to use mastic in my *sfeeha* dough – it's expensive and not really necessary – but I wouldn't want to miss out on that taste memory every time I take a bite of the savoury little pies.

SPINACH PIE FILLING

FATAYER BIL SABANIKH

If you like your filling very lemony, use the optional lemon sea salt because most of the lemon juice is squeezed from the spinach when it is drained. This filling can be made a day in advance; cover tightly and refrigerate.

MAKES ENOUGH FOR 8 X 20CM PIES OR 60 X 7.5CM PIES

2 red onions, diced
½ teaspoon sea salt, plus extra to taste
1.5kg fresh or frozen spinach, thawed, if necessary, and chopped
2 tablespoons sumac
½ teaspoon freshly ground black pepper
½ teaspoon lemon salt (optional)
pinch of crushed red chilli flakes (optional)
150g whole walnuts (optional)
125ml extra virgin olive oil
juice of 2 lemons

Combine the onions and sea salt in a bowl and, using your hands, rub the onions until they soften and begin to release their water. Squeeze the onions of all their liquid, then transfer them to a large bowl and add the spinach. Rub the onions and spinach in your hands until the spinach softens and wilts and squeeze as much liquid from the spinach as possible.

Add the sumac, pepper, lemon salt, if using, red chilli flakes, walnuts, if using, olive oil and lemon juice to the large bowl and mix together with your hands until the seasonings are thoroughly incorporated. Transfer to a sieve to drain off all the liquid (the dough will not adhere if there is any excess) and taste and adjust the sea salt, if necessary.

CHEESE PIE FILLING

FATAYER BIL JIBIN

MAKES ENOUGH FOR 8 X 20CM PIES OR 60 X 7.5CM PIES

750g feta cheese, diced
4 plum tomatoes or 2 beefsteak tomatoes, diced
1 medium white onion, diced
90g chopped fresh green za'atar, or 3 tablespoons dried
120ml extra virgin olive oil, plus extra to taste
juice of 1 lemon

In a large bowl, combine the cheese and tomatoes with the onion, za'atar, oil and lemon juice. Mix together with your hands until thoroughly incorporated.

❧ BIG-BATCH BAKING

I generally make double batches of *sfeeha* and put some in the freezer, where they will keep for up to 3 months. If you are planning to freeze, bake the pies for 15–20 minutes, then leave them to cool on a wire rack. Pack them in airtight containers with greaseproof paper separating the layers. To serve, thaw the pies at room temperature for 2–3 hours, then bake in a preheated oven at 200°C/gas mark 6 until heated through, about 10 minutes.

ARABIC BREAD

— ❖ —

KMAJ

When I was growing up, my mother made 40–50 loaves of this at one time. She would spread a huge piece of fabric in the bedroom and set the shaped discs of dough to rest on it – far from the constant activity in other parts of the house, where it ran the risk of being sat on or buried under books and bags! When I was very young, everyone brought their bread to the village oven to be baked, but eventually, private homes had their own ovens – along with those intoxicating aromas. Fresh baked bread is a special treat; if you don't have the time to prepare it, buy good-quality packaged bread in Middle Eastern or specialist markets.

🕯 **COOKING TIP** The dough can be made ahead and frozen for up to 3 months. Wrap it in greaseproof paper and place it in a resealable plastic bag. Thaw at room temperature before shaping into discs. If you are making this for the Chicken 'Pizza' (page 142), be sure to place a drop of olive oil on each piece and tap all over with your fingertips. This will prevent the bread from splitting open.

In a small bowl, combine 120ml warm water with the yeast and sugar, stirring every few minutes until the yeast dissolves and begins to foam, about 5 minutes.

Into a large bowl, sift together the flour, powdered milk, if using, and salt. Make a well in the centre and pour in the yeast mixture, the remaining warm water, the olive oil and the yogurt, if using. Using a fork, mix the flour mixture into the yeast mixture, working from the outside in until thoroughly incorporated. Alternatively, put all of the ingredients in the bowl of a freestanding mixer fitted with the dough hook. Mix on medium speed for 10–12 minutes, or until the dough pulls away from the sides of the bowl and is hanging entirely on the hook.

MAKES 12

620ml warm water
4½ teaspoons dried yeast
1 tablespoon sugar
750g plain flour or wholewheat flour, or 375g of each, plus extra for dusting
50g powdered milk or 250ml plain yogurt
1 tablespoon sea salt
250ml extra virgin olive oil, plus extra for greasing

Knead the dough in the bowl until it's soft yet slightly sticky, about 5 minutes. Add a drop of olive oil on top of the dough and turn it over in the bowl. Cover with a tea towel and place in the warmest part of the kitchen until it doubles in size, about 30 minutes–1 hour.

Line a baking sheet with greaseproof paper and rub with a thin coat of oil. Knock the dough back, then pull off pieces the size of oranges. Working with one piece at a time, fold the dough onto itself, then gather it up so that it looks like a money bag. Grab the dough above the cinched portion and roll the dough ball around until the underside is completely smooth and is the size and shape of a hamburger bun. Place the ball, smooth-side up, onto the greaseproof paper and continue with the remaining dough. Leave it to rest for 20 minutes; the dough will expand slightly.

Preheat the oven to 230°C/gas mark 8 and grease 2 baking sheets with oil. Dust a clean work surface with flour. Roll out each piece of dough into a 23cm round and, working in batches, transfer these to the prepared baking sheets and leave to rest for a few minutes. Bake until the bottom is golden brown, 5–7 minutes. Serve warm.

ZA'ATAR BREAD

— ◆ —

MANAKEESH

There's nothing quite like eating this aromatic flatbread warm, straight from the oven. Growing up, it was always on the weekday breakfast table. *Manakeesh* is found all over the Middle East, sold out of street carts. The vendor spoons mint and tomatoes onto the *manooshi*, rolls it all up into a cone, wraps it in a piece of greaseproof paper and, if you are lucky, presents it with a big smile.

Normally, I like to make both the za'atar and red pepper and onion topping (see opposite) so I have an equal amount of each type of flatbread.

⚜ **COOKING TIP** The dough can be made ahead and frozen for up to 3 months. Wrap it in greaseproof paper and place it in a resealable plastic bag. Alternatively, wrap the baked and cooled *manakeesh* in two layers of cling film and freeze for up to 4 months. To reheat, remove the cling film, wrap in aluminium foil and bake at 175°C/gas mark 4 until heated through.

Prepare the Arabic bread up to the point where it is resting on the baking sheets. Using your fingertips, make indentations in the dough. Alternatively, make a raised rim by pinching the perimeter of the dough as if crimping the crust of a pie.

In a medium bowl, combine the za'atar and olive oil and stir until thoroughly combined.

Spread each disc with za'atar topping to coat and bake until the bottom is golden brown, 5–7 minutes. Serve warm.

MAKES 12 FLATBREADS

Arabic Bread (page 57)
1 quantity za'atar with sesame seeds
250ml extra virgin olive oil
vegetable oil, for greasing

RED PEPPER AND ONION FLATBREAD

KHUBZ BIL FILFIL

Wafa's sister Ikbal is known within the family for making the very best *khubz bil filfil*. She makes it the traditional way – in an outdoor clay oven known as a taboun, which gives the dough the perfect char. To this day, she bakes it dressed in a traditional housecoat and headscarf trimmed in crocheted flowers known as a *mandeel*. She has worn the same one ever since I can remember, and whenever she ties her *mandeel* on, we all know warm bread is in the offing.

⚜ COOKING TIP If you're a purist, use lemon juice, but I have found that substituting lemon salt ensures that the dough will not be overly moist and sticky.

Prepare the Arabic bread up to the point where it is resting on the baking sheets. Using your fingertips, make indentations in the dough. Alternatively, make a raised rim by pinching the perimeter of the dough as if crimping the crust of a pie.

In a medium bowl, combine the chilli paste, onion and tomatoes with the oil, lemon juice, sesame seeds, cumin and salt. Stir to thoroughly incorporate.

Spread each disc with the onion mixture and bake until the bottom is golden brown, 5–7 minutes. Serve warm.

MAKES 12 FLATBREADS

Arabic Bread (page 57)
250ml seedless Middle Eastern or Turkish chilli paste
1 medium white onion, diced
2 plum tomatoes, peeled and grated, juices reserved
120ml extra virgin olive oil
juice of 1 lemon or ⅓ teaspoon lemon salt
100g unhulled sesame seeds (shells on)
½ teaspoon ground cumin
½ teaspoon sea salt, or to taste

SAVOURY PIES

SAMBOSEK

A staple on every mezze spread, these little half-moons are made with unleavened dough that results in a wonderfully crispy texture when fried. A forgiving and versatile dough, it can be flavoured with onion or garlic powder, any dried herb, caraway or black nigella seeds. The fillings below are those on the Tanoreen menu, but you can just as easily make simple cheese pies using crumbled feta and za'atar, grated halloumi or goat's cheese. Serve the pies on a platter alongside my homemade Thick Tahini Sauce and Hot Sauce (pages 195 and 194). Or try them with my Basil Pesto (page 191).

In a large bowl, combine the flour, water, oil, sugar and salt. Using a wooden spoon, stir until the mixture comes together. Turn out onto a clean work surface dusted with flour and knead until the dough is tender. Alternatively, combine the ingredients in the bowl of a freestanding mixer fitted with the dough hook and beat on medium speed until the dough is tender. Shape into a ball, cover with a tea towel and leave to rest for 10 minutes.

Pull off a piece of dough about the size of an orange. Lightly dust a rolling pin with flour and roll out the dough as thinly as possible. Using a 5cm biscuit cutter, cut out circles in the dough.

Spoon 1 tablespoon of the meat or vegetable filling onto one side of the circle, leaving a 6mm rim exposed around the perimeter. Fold the circle in half to make a half moon. Using a fork, crimp the edges to seal them. Repeat with the remaining dough. At this point, the pies can be sealed tightly in an airtight container and frozen up to 2 months.

Fill a frying pan with 1.2cm of oil and place over a high heat until hot. Working in batches and without crowding the pan, fry the *sambosek*, turning once, until both sides are golden, about 4 minutes in total. Using a slotted spoon, transfer the pies to a kitchen-paper–lined tray to drain.

MAKES 24 PIES

500g plain flour, plus extra for dusting
500ml water
60ml extra virgin olive oil
1 teaspoon sugar
1 teaspoon sea salt
Meat or Vegetable Filling (opposite)
vegetable oil, for frying

MEAT FILLING

60ml extra virgin olive oil
1 small red onion, chopped
6 garlic cloves, finely chopped
1 chilli, deseeded and diced (optional)
1 teaspoon ground coriander
1 teaspoon ground allspice
1 teaspoon ground cumin
½ teaspoon freshly ground black pepper
1kg chopped lamb meat from the leg or
    lean beef such as sirloin
2 tablespoons pomegranate molasses
juice of 1 lemon
2 teaspoons sea salt
75g slivered almonds, toasted
75g pine nuts, toasted

Heat the oil in a medium frying pan over a medium-high heat and sauté the onion until soft and translucent, about 3 minutes. Stir in the garlic until fragrant and golden, and then the chilli, if using, until softened. Add the coriander, allspice, cumin and black pepper and count to five. Increase the heat to high, add the lamb and sauté until the meat is cooked through, 7–10 minutes. Stir in the pomegranate molasses, lemon juice and salt. Add the almonds and pine nuts and mix until well incorporated. Remove from the heat and set aside.

VEGETABLE FILLING

MAKES ENOUGH FOR 24 PIES

6 tablespoons extra virgin olive oil
3 shallots, diced
3 garlic cloves, finely chopped
3 medium baking potatoes, diced
1 tablespoon ground coriander
1 teaspoon ground cumin
1 teaspoon freshly ground black pepper
30g chopped fresh coriander
1 green chilli, deseeded and cut into small dice
    (optional)
375g frozen baby peas
juice of 1 lemon, or to taste
2 tablespoons pomegranate molasses
1 teaspoon ground turmeric
1 teaspoon sea salt
pinch of saffron (optional)

Heat the oil in a large frying pan over a medium-high heat. When hot, sauté the shallots until soft and fragrant, 3–4 minutes, then add the garlic and stir for a further minute. Add the potatoes and cook until they begin to colour, about 5 minutes. Stir in the ground coriander, cumin and black pepper and count to five. Tip in the fresh coriander and chilli and cook until the coriander colours, about 1 minute. Stir in the peas for 3–5 minutes, then add the lemon juice, pomegranate molasses, turmeric, salt and saffron, if using, and sauté for a further minute. Taste and adjust the seasonings and lemon juice, as desired.

SALADS

ESSENTIAL SIDE NOTES

Salads in the Middle Eastern tradition are invariably served alongside every meal, essential keynotes, unlike in Europe and the US, where they rarely make it to the centre of the plate. No matter what the composition or ingredients, salads are always on the table as an accompaniment, part of a mezze spread or a side dish.

What's more, the definition of a Middle Eastern salad is quite loose – it can be composed of leafy greens and vegetables as in Fattoush (page 70); a preponderance of herbs tossed with a few grains as in Tabbouleh (page 73); or a mix of very finely chopped vegetables in a thick spicy sauce, somewhat like a chutney, as in Turkish Salad (page 45). This condiment-like salad is perfect for slathering on grilled Chicken Kebabs (page 146) and is a suitable counterpoint for hummus on a mezze spread. I often suggest that my customers order the Cauliflower Salad (page 75), tossed in a pomegranate-tahini sauce, as part of a mezze platter rather than as a side dish; it is as hearty and earthy as a main course, making it a lovely addition to an assortment of small dishes. Other salads are served as the yin to a main course's yang. One of my favourites is the easy-to-make Tomato Salad (page 69), which is as ubiquitous on the Middle Eastern table as the green salad is in the US. It's tossed in a lemony vinaigrette and typically served as a cooling counterpoint to rich dishes such as Spiced Lamb Shank (page 164) and earthy *Mujadara* (page 178).

However you choose to enjoy the salads that follow, do as I do and season them to suit yourself. All of the spices, herbs, oils, vinegars and other flavourings can be adjusted according to your taste. I am an avowed lover of the brightening power of lemon juice, so I tend to use it quite liberally. If you love the earthy flavour nutmeg lends a dish, grind a pinch more. Add chilli paste gradually to a vinaigrette, tasting as you go until you reach the heat level you're after. As with every other course on the Middle Eastern table, salads are prepared with care, respect and attention because they are an integral part of each and every meal.

'NO MATTER THE COMPOSITION OR INGREDIENTS, SALADS ARE ALWAYS ON THE TABLE AS AN ACCOMPANIMENT, PART OF A MEZZE SPREAD OR A SIDE DISH.'

AUBERGINE SALAD

— ◆•◆ —

SALATET BAITENJAN

One of the first things I make myself when I go home to Nazareth is the aubergine sandwich we often ate on Friday afternoons when I was growing up. I always dressed mine with tomato slices and a simple sauce of garlic, lemon juice and olive oil. Perfection. This salad, a staple on the Tanoreen menu, is inspired by that beloved sandwich. It is excellent with *Mujadara* (page 178) or Falafel (page 52) tucked into a sandwich.

Preheat the oven to 250°C/gas mark 9. Divide the aubergine pieces between two baking sheets and brush them all over with olive oil. Sprinkle with the salt and bake until the aubergines are lightly browned and softened, 20–30 minutes. Set aside to cool.

In a large mixing bowl, combine the tomatoes, green and red peppers, parsley, olives, shallots, onion, garlic, lemon juice, 6 tablespoons oil and red chilli flakes, if using. Using a wooden spoon, stir to mix thoroughly. Taste and adjust the lemon juice and salt.

Gently fold in the cooled aubergine, distributing it evenly and taking care not to crush it. Transfer to a platter and serve.

SERVES 4–6

3 medium–large aubergines (1.5–2kg in total), skin on, cut into large dice

6 tablespoons extra virgin olive oil, plus extra for brushing the aubergine

1 teaspoon sea salt, or to taste

8 plum tomatoes, cut into small dice, or 3 beefsteak tomatoes, cut into large dice

1 medium green pepper, deseeded and diced

1 medium red pepper, deseeded and diced

60g chopped fresh flat-leaf parsley

75g Kalamata or green olives, pitted and chopped

3 shallots, 1 medium red onion or 6 spring onions, white parts only, chopped

6–8 garlic cloves, crushed

juice of 3 lemons, or to taste

½ teaspoon red chilli flakes (optional)

TOMATO SALAD

—◦•◦—

SALATET BANDOORA

This is one of the most popular salads on the Palestinian table. You would be hard pressed to find a single household in the region that doesn't serve a tomato salad with every dinner during the summer months. I prepare it the traditional and very simple way: tomatoes, onions and chillies. However, it is not unusual to find diced cucumber and chopped parsley in some preparations. It is a colourful addition to the mezze table and is also eaten with anything grilled, Fried Fish (page 129) and Rice and Vermicelli Pilaf (page 182). For the best results, use ripe summer tomatoes at their peak.

In a medium serving bowl, combine the tomatoes, onions and chilli with the mint, garlic, oil, lemon juice and salt. Toss thoroughly to combine. Taste and adjust the oil, lemon juice and salt, and serve.

SERVES 4–6

3–4 beefsteak tomatoes or 8 plum tomatoes, peeled and diced, at room temperature
2 small red or white onions, diced
1 chilli (jalapeño or long green or red), deseeded and cut into small dice
4½ teaspoons chopped fresh mint or 1 tablespoon dried
½ teaspoon finely chopped garlic
120ml extra virgin olive oil, or to taste
4–6 tablespoons fresh lemon juice, or to taste
½ teaspoon sea salt, or to taste

BEETROOT SALAD

—◦•◦—

SALATET SHAMANDAR

In the Middle East, the most popular ways to prepare beetroot are pickled with turnips (page 188) or as my father used to do, boiled with carrots and dipped in sugar for a quick, old-style dessert.

**   The beetroot salad I created at Tanoreen is the perfect example of how travel has influenced my palate over the years – in this case, time spent in Italy. I add a cheese-free basil pesto and roasted slivered almonds and walnuts to the beetroot. Sometimes I dot the top with some goats' cheese just before serving.**

Place the beetroot in a large pot with enough cold water to cover. Bring to the boil, reduce the heat and simmer until fork tender, 20–40 minutes. Transfer to a colander to drain. When cool enough to handle, slice the beetroot across into 6mm-thick slices.

Meanwhile, in a large bowl, add the oil, lemon juice and pesto with the garlic, basil, mint, walnuts, almonds and salt and whisk to combine.

Tip the beetroot into the bowl and toss to coat. Transfer to a shallow dish and serve.

SERVES 6

1kg medium beetroots, scrubbed and peeled
120ml extra virgin olive oil
80ml fresh lemon juice
80ml Basil Pesto (page 191)
1½ teaspoons finely chopped garlic
30g chopped fresh basil
30g chopped fresh mint
75g chopped walnuts, toasted
50g slivered almonds, toasted
1½ teaspoons sea salt

FATTOUSH SALAD

This superb salad is very popular throughout the Middle East, but especially throughout the Levantine. Every country has its own version, but, honestly, I think the most delicious version comes from Lebanon. Some won't consider fattoush the real thing without sumac; others say purslane is the essential ingredient. I agree that both are important components (but don't worry about the purslane if you can't find it); however, the one ingredient that makes fattoush, well, fattoush, is plenty of toasted Arabic bread!

⚜ INGREDIENT NOTE In my mind, the fattoush my mother composed was the best: She just tossed in whatever the garden yielded. The ingredients must all be cut into the same size pieces – about 6mm dice – and tossed with sumac, dried mint and toasted pitta. Otherwise, the sky is the limit! I add fresh pomegranate seeds when they are readily available or finely chopped Granny Smith apples. If heirloom tomatoes are in season, I use them. You can use whatever fresh greens are to hand, too. You see where this is going!

In a large salad bowl, combine the lettuce, tomatoes, cucumbers, onion, spring onions, garlic and mint. Gently toss together.

In a lidded jar, combine the lemon juice, oil, sumac, garlic, mint and salt. Screw the lid on tightly and shake to mix.

Just before serving, drizzle the dressing over the salad and garnish with the toasted bread chips.

VARIATION *One of my favourite versions of fattoush is a mix of rocket, coriander, spring onions and radishes tossed with toasted Arabic bread and the dressing above.*

SERVES 8

180g chopped Romaine lettuce
3 plum tomatoes, chopped
3 small cucumbers, chopped
1 medium red onion, chopped
3 spring onions, chopped
1 garlic clove, crushed
8 fresh mint leaves, chopped
Arabic Bread (page 57), toasted and
   broken up, for serving

For the Dressing
180ml fresh lemon juice
120ml extra virgin olive oil
2 tablespoons sumac
1 garlic clove, crushed
2 teaspoons dried mint
1½ teaspoons sea salt

DRYING HERBS

If you grow your own leafy herbs (mint, parsley, oregano, thyme or basil) or have bought more than you can use immediately, you can dry them. Pick the leaves off the stems and wash them thoroughly in several changes of cold water, each time lifting the herbs out of the water (don't pour them out or you won't get rid of the dirt). Dry completely in a tea towel you reserve for herbs. Spread on a baking sheet and slide into a very low oven (130°C/gas mark 1) for 1 hour, turning once to ensure even drying. Alternatively, set them out in full sun for a full day, turning once to ensure even drying. Store the dried herbs in a Mason jar or other glass container with a tight-fitting lid. The herbs should keep their aroma and flavour for many months.

FETA SALAD

—◆—

SALATET FETA

Fresh green za'atar, also known in the Middle East as wild thyme, has been a staple in the region's cuisine since medieval times. It is rare to find it here, though I have noticed it showing up in some of the larger supermarkets. Though the flavour of the salad will be different if you use dried za'atar, which is available in Middle Eastern markets and online, it is no less delicious.

This salad started out as a classic za'atar salad – tomatoes, za'atar, lemon juice and olive oil – which I made for my daughter, Jumana, throughout her childhood. But I took a cue from the Lebanese, who often add feta, which lends a salty flavour and creamy texture.

❖ **COOKING TIPS** I use Greek feta whenever possible; it's firmer and easier to cut into clean dice than the creamier French version. Garnish with the onions rather than tossing them into the salad. That way, when you are storing leftovers or making the dish ahead, simply remove the onions from the top and keep the salad tightly covered, in the fridge, for up to three days.

In a medium serving bowl, combine the feta and tomatoes with the za'atar, red chilli flakes, if using, oil, lemon juice and salt to taste. Gently toss to combine.

Taste and adjust the oil, lemon juice and salt. Scatter the onions on top and serve with warm Arabic bread.

SERVES 6–8

500g feta, preferably Greek, cut into
    1.2cm dice
8 plum tomatoes or 4–5 beefsteak
    tomatoes, diced
60g chopped fresh green za'atar or fresh
    oregano leaves or 30g dried za'atar
    or oregano
½ teaspoon red chilli flakes (optional)
120ml extra virgin olive oil, or to taste
juice of 1½ lemons, or to taste
sea salt, to taste
1 small red onion, chopped (optional)
Arabic Bread (page 57), for serving

TABBOULEH

Tabbouleh is an essential part of a classic mezze spread, but it is also a very popular lunch dish. When I was growing up, tabbouleh was only prepared by women and eaten by women. Of course, these days you will find everyone – men, women, children – eating tabbouleh – not only in the Middle East but all over the West. It is synonymous with a healthy diet, touted for parsley's nutritious profile. Stateside, it is often served with Arabic bread, a pairing you will never find in the Middle East. Instead, try eating tabbouleh in lettuce cups or wrapped in fresh-off-the-plant vine leaves if you are lucky enough to have access to them. As with many classic dishes, every region has its own version of tabbouleh; Nazarenes put a pinch of cumin, Lebanese add extra bulgur (you can double or triple the amount used below if you like). Tabbouleh should be tossed just before serving, as it has a tendency to wilt rather quickly. I don't recommend making it ahead or planning for leftovers.

COOKING TIPS There's nothing quite like freshly made tabbouleh prepared with the fluffiest parsley and top-quality olive oil. The trick to featherweight parsley is not only to make sure it is thoroughly dry before chopping, but to resist over chopping, which bruises the soft herb. I prefer flat-leaf parsley to its curly-leaved cousin, which, though easier to chop, is not as soft or flavourful as the flat-leaf version.

In a large bowl, combine the parsley with half the tomatoes, the onion or spring onions, fresh and dried mint, salt, lemon juice, oil and cracked wheat. Gently toss the ingredients together, then taste and adjust the lemon juice and salt.

Transfer to a serving bowl and garnish with the remaining tomatoes. Serve over the lettuce, cabbage leaves or vine leaves.

VARIATIONS *To make tabbouleh the Nazarene way, add 50g peeled, chopped cucumber and 1 teaspoon ground cumin. If you are allergic to wheat, skip the bulgur altogether and add a chopped cucumber and chilli pepper to give the salad both crunch and a sharp bite.*

SERVES 4

240g fresh flat-leaf parsley

2½ plum tomatoes, chopped

1 medium red onion or 6 spring onions, chopped

2 tablespoons chopped fresh mint

1 tablespoon dried mint

½ tablespoon sea salt, or to taste

juice of 2 lemons, or to taste

80–120ml good-quality extra virgin olive oil

3–4 tablespoons very fine cracked wheat (bulgur), picked over and rinsed

Romaine lettuce, cabbage leaves or vine leaves, for serving

CAULIFLOWER SALAD

— ◆ —

SALATET ZAHRA

In Nazareth, cauliflower is prepared and eaten simply: fried and tucked into Arabic bread, spritzed with lemon juice and sprinkled with sea salt. That elemental sandwich inspired this dish, which is dressed with a pomegranate molasses-spiked tahini sauce. It's a beloved mezze on the Tanoreen menu, and I also serve it as a main dish with meat or chicken.

Place the cauliflower in a large saucepan with enough water to cover. Bring the water to the boil and cook for 2 minutes. Transfer to a colander to drain.

Place 1.2–2cm oil in a large frying pan over a high heat. When hot and working in batches, fry the cauliflower until golden brown, about 2 minutes per side. Using a slotted spoon, transfer to kitchen paper to drain. Alternatively, preheat the oven to 250°C/gas mark 9. Spread the cauliflower on a baking sheet and brush all over with oil. Roast until golden and fork tender, about 15 minutes.

Arrange the cauliflower on a serving dish. Drizzle with the tahini sauce, followed by the pomegranate molasses, then garnish with parsley and serve.

SERVES 6–8

2 heads cauliflower, cut into 5cm florets
vegetable oil, for frying
250ml Thick Tahini Sauce (page 195)
60ml pomegranate molasses
2 tablespoons chopped fresh flat-leaf parsley, for garnish

TANOREEN POTATO SALAD

— ◆ —

SALATET BATATA

This is made dozens of ways back home – dressed with mayonnaise or tahini or, in this case, with a garlic and lemon combination warmed with cumin and cooled with mint. It's a hybrid of the way my mother used to make potato salad and the version I created for Tanoreen. The traditional recipe, made all over Palestine, Lebanon and Syria, features the first six ingredients. I love the addition of olives; they lend a wonderful sea salty, briny kick.

Place the potatoes in a large saucepan with enough water to cover. Bring to the boil and cook over a medium-high heat until a cocktail stick slides easily into a piece but doesn't cause the potato to fall apart, 7–10 minutes. Transfer to a colander to drain, then rinse under cold water. Spread the potatoes on a baking sheet to cool.

Combine the garlic and salt in the bottom of a mixing bowl. Using a fork, mash the garlic into a paste. Add the oil and lemon juice with the parsley, spring onions, green and red peppers, mint, cumin, paprika and black pepper; mix to combine. Tip in the potatoes and, using a wooden spoon, toss gently until thoroughly coated with the dressing. Transfer to a serving dish and garnish with the olives and the coriander.

SERVES 6

15 small red potatoes, in 2.5cm dice
2 tablespoons chopped garlic
1 tablespoon sea salt
120ml extra virgin olive oil
juice of 2 lemons
80g chopped flat-leaf parsley
6 spring onions, green parts only, chopped
30g finely diced green pepper
30g finely diced red pepper
2 tablespoons chopped fresh mint
1 teaspoon ground cumin
1 teaspoon ground paprika
1 teaspoon freshly ground black pepper
50g chopped green olives for garnish
3 tablespoons chopped coriander, for garnish

TANOREEN GREEN SALAD

———— •✦• ————

I created this Tanoreen speciality for customers who were looking for a tossed green salad option. Here, a mix of baby greens is tossed with a dressing that borrows flavourful ingredients from all over the world: sesame oil, ginger and pomegranate molasses. It is an unusual combination that really hits the mark. You can mix and match your greens, but I find peppery rocket is essential here.

In a large serving bowl, combine the rocket, spinach, lettuce and kale with the tomatoes, onion and mint leaves; toss to mix.

In a large bowl, whisk together the lemon juice, sesame oil, pomegranate molasses, if using, olive oil, garlic and ginger.

When ready to serve, pour the dressing over the salad and toss to coat the greens evenly. Season with salt and sprinkle the olives and walnuts, if using, on top.

SERVES 6–8

240g rocket
240g baby spinach
80g small-leaf lettuce
80g finely chopped kale
2 plum tomatoes, diced, or 12 cherry
    tomatoes, halved
1 red onion, diced
8–10 fresh mint leaves
50g chopped green olives
75g chopped walnuts (optional)

For the Dressing
250ml fresh lemon juice
3 tablespoons toasted sesame oil
2 tablespoons pomegranate molasses
    (optional)
3 tablespoons extra virgin olive oil
3 garlic cloves, finely chopped
1 teaspoon freshly grated ginger
sea salt, to taste

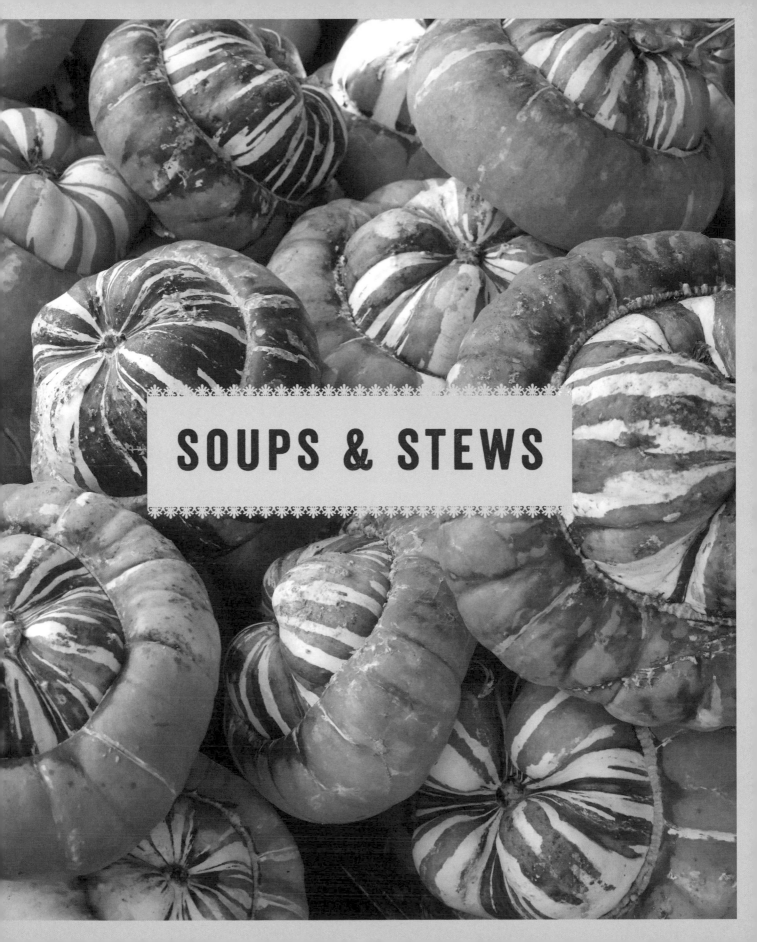

SOUPS & STEWS

FAMILY MEALS

Soups and stews, or *yakhani* as they are known in the Middle East, are synonymous with family meals. When I was growing up in Nazareth, dishes centred around beef or lamb were generally reserved for special celebrations, holidays and weddings, as meat was too expensive to serve a family of seven every night. Let's face it, it still is.

My mother was masterful at creating hearty, healthy soups and stews made primarily with vegetables; meat was always a secondary ingredient. She could turn such humble garden bounty as cauliflower, runner beans, okra and potatoes into soups and stews that always seemed special. Her secret was actually quite simple: fresh ingredients, seasoned well and cooked with care. I have very fond memories of her grinding down the freshly harvested freekeh (smoked wheat) into a coarse crumb and turning it into a dinner soup with a bit of chicken or lamb. Whenever I make Freekeh Soup (page 91), the aroma of warm spices and smoky grains never ceases to lift my spirits.

I cook for my family here in the States much the same way my mother did, with soups and stews routinely simmering on the hob. They make sense not just for a large family like the one I grew up in, but for my decidedly smaller family of four. Indeed, my son, Tarek, would rather eat stew than anything else for any meal, especially breakfast. When he visits, I make sure to have the fridge fully stocked with his favourites: Cauliflower and Lamb Stew (page 98) and Chopped Mlookhia Stew (page 99).

The soups in this chapter are ideal for preparing in big batches and freezing. What's more, once all of the ingredients make it into the pot, they will cook slowly to allow the flavours of the seasoned stock, vegetables and, in some cases, meat or chicken, to meld. The active cooking time in these recipes is actually quite short. As with most stews and soups, they taste better the day after, making them ideal make-ahead meals.

In the beef- and chicken-based soups, it is ideal to use Seasoned Chicken with Stock (page 90) and Seasoned Lamb or Beef with Stock (page 102). Both are fragrant with cardamom, nutmeg and allspice, which lends a distinct Middle Eastern flavour to any dish that calls for them. Of course, if time is not on your side, good-quality shop-bought stocks are fine.

All of the soups in this chapter are hearty enough to be meals in themselves. Ladle the stews over Rice and Vermicelli Pilaf (page 182), or serve bowls of the soups or stews with warm Arabic bread (page 57) and some olives, pickles and fresh sliced jalapeños on the side. At Tanoreen, come autumn and winter, I always make sure to offer a few more of these robust options on my menu, as they warm up my diners on those infamously cold New York winter nights.

'I COOK FOR MY FAMILY HERE IN THE STATES MUCH THE SAME WAY MY MOTHER DID, WITH SOUPS AND STEWS ROUTINELY SIMMERING ON THE HOB. THEY MAKE SENSE NOT JUST FOR A LARGE FAMILY LIKE THE ONE I GREW UP IN, BUT FOR MY DECIDEDLY SMALLER FAMILY OF FOUR.'

TANOREEN'S LEEK AND POTATO SOUP

I had never tasted leeks until I arrived in New York – we didn't grow them in Nazareth, but instead used spring onions. Cooking with these mild members of the onion family seemed like an interesting prospect, but as you probably know by now, I am hard-pressed to make anything with too mellow a flavour. So I punched up this classic soup with elements from the earthy Middle Eastern flavour profile. To give the soup a little bite, add the chopped white parts of six spring onions.

COOKING TIP Take care not to allow the shallots and garlic to burn; they will darken this white soup.

Place the oil in a large stockpot over a medium heat and sauté the shallots until tender but still pale, 4–5 minutes. Stir in the garlic until fragrant but still pale, about 2 minutes, then the pepper, nutmeg and cardamom, about 30 seconds. Add the potatoes and leeks and sauté until thoroughly combined. Season with salt, reduce the heat to medium-low, cover and cook, stirring occasionally, until the potatoes are fork-tender, about 15 minutes.

Add the milk and cream, if using, increase the heat to high and bring to the boil. Reduce the heat and simmer for 15 minutes, scraping the sides of the pot frequently with a rubber spatula. Add the ghee and sage, if using, and stir for 2 minutes. Remove from the heat and purée the soup with a stick blender.

Ladle into bowls, garnish with nutmeg and serve with toasted Arabic bread.

SERVES 6–8

120ml extra virgin olive oil
4 shallots, chopped
1 tablespoon finely chopped garlic
½ teaspoon freshly ground white or black pepper
½ teaspoon ground nutmeg, plus extra for garnish (optional)
⅓ teaspoon ground cardamom (optional)
6 baking potatoes, peeled and diced
6–8 leeks, light green and white parts only, thoroughly rinsed and chopped
1 tablespoon sea salt
2 litres full-fat or skimmed milk
240ml double cream (optional)
3 tablespoons ghee or butter
1 fresh sage leaf (optional)
Arabic Bread (page 57), toasted

TOMATO AND SQUASH SOUP

—◆—

SHORABIT BANDOORA

It may not be wise to fiddle with an American classic – but this was one of the first soups I experimented with when I moved to New York. Inspired by the tomato sauce in which my mother cooked her Stuffed Aubergine and Squash (page 150), this recipe uses these same components, in a new way. I use all three vegetables – the squash and aubergine give the soup both body and a subtle sweetness, and of course the tomatoes provide the delicious crimson base. I prefer a thicker soup; it should cling nicely to a piece of bread. But you can thin the soup with water or broth to the desired consistency. I often float a thick slab of fried halloumi in each bowl and always serve toasted Arabic bread or, even better, garlic bread on the side. This is delicious cold, hot and the day after you make it.

Place the oil in a large saucepan over a medium heat and sauté the shallots until soft and fragrant, about 4 minutes. Stir in the garlic until fragrant, about 1 minute, then the coriander, salt and pepper, 30 seconds. Add the chopped basil and oregano and cook for 1 minute, then reduce the heat, tip in the squash and aubergine and cook, covered, until the vegetables are soft, stirring occasionally, 3–5 minutes. Add the sugar or lemon juice, fresh tomatoes and tomato purée (or the tinned chopped tomatoes), cover and cook until the tomatoes are soft, about 15 minutes.

Remove the pan from the heat and, using a stick blender, purée until smooth. If the soup is too thick, gradually add up to 750ml tomato juice or water to achieve the desired consistency.

Serve hot or at room temperature, garnished with the basil and/or oregano leaves with Arabic or garlic bread on the side.

SERVES 6–8

120ml extra virgin olive oil

3 shallots, chopped

3–4 garlic cloves, finely chopped

1 teaspoon coriander

1 teaspoon sea salt, or to taste

1 teaspoon freshly ground black pepper

60g chopped basil, plus a few whole leaves, for garnish

15g chopped oregano, plus a few whole leaves, for garnish

4 Arabic squash or marrows, skin on, or 2 small courgettes, peeled and chopped

3–4 Italian baby aubergines, peeled and chopped

½ teaspoon sugar or 3 tablespoons fresh lemon juice (optional)

10 large tomatoes or 15 plum tomatoes, chopped (reserve juices) or 2 (400g) tins chopped tomatoes

1 tablespoon tomato purée (if using fresh tomato only)

750ml tomato juice or water (optional)

Arabic Bread (page 57), toasted, or garlic bread, for serving

83

LENTIL NOODLE SOUP WITH KALE

—— ◆ ——

RUSHTAY

This hearty Palestinian soup is more commonly prepared by West Bank cooks than by those in Galilee; I learned how to make it from friends I met in Jerusalem. It is a meal in itself and a favourite among vegetarian patrons of Tanoreen. If you don't have one of the greens on hand, just substitute more of the others. Don't skip the squeeze of lemon near the end – it transforms the soup. Stirring in the garlicky *Teklai* (page 196) at the very end gives the soup a bit more intensity. Serve it with a few olives.

Combine the lentils and a pinch of salt in a saucepan and cover with water by 2.5cm. Cover with the lid and boil over a high heat for 20 minutes. Drain and set aside.

Place the olive oil in a large saucepan over a medium-high heat and sauté the onions or shallots, and chilli, if using, until golden brown, 7–10 minutes. Stir in the garlic until fragrant, about 2 minutes, then the cumin, coriander and black pepper, about 30 seconds. Tip in the celery, carrots and fresh coriander, then cover and cook for 5 minutes. Add the spinach, kale, tomatoes, if using, 3.75 litres water and the remaining 1 tablespoon salt and bring to the boil. Reduce the heat, cover and simmer for 20 minutes.

Add the lentils, return the stock to a simmer and cook for a further 10 minutes. Add the fettuccine and cook until al dente. Stir in the lemon juice followed by the *teklai*, if using. Serve hot.

VARIATION *For a gluten-free version, cut six 20cm corn tortillas into 1.2cm strips and use in place of the fettuccine or use gluten-free pasta.*

SERVES 8–10

660g brown lentils
1 tablespoon plus a pinch of sea salt
250ml olive oil
3 medium red or white onions or
   5 large shallots, diced
1 long chilli, deseeded and diced (optional)
6 garlic cloves, finely chopped
4½ teaspoons ground cumin
4½ teaspoons ground coriander
1 tablespoon freshly ground black pepper
4 sticks of celery, diced
2 large carrots, peeled and diced
80g chopped fresh coriander
160g chopped fresh spinach
160g chopped kale
2 green or plum tomatoes, diced (optional)
225g fettuccine, broken in half
juice of 2 lemons
1 tablespoon *Teklai* (page 196; optional)

PURÉED LENTIL SOUP

SHORABIT ADDAS MAJROOSH

A staple in the Palestinian region, this soup could not be more comforting, healthy or simple to make. Because the lentils are rich in protein and fibre, and the soup is thick, I have served it for dinner with only a side salad to complete the meal.

In a large stockpot, heat the oil over a medium heat and sauté the onions and garlic until golden brown, about 4 minutes. Stir in the coriander, cumin and pepper and heat until fragrant for 1 minute. Add the carrots and cook until soft, about 5 minutes. Pour in 3–3.75 litres water and the lentils and bring to the boil. Reduce the heat and simmer for 30 minutes, or until the lentils are easily crushed when pressed against the side of the pot.

Stir in the lemon juice, season with the salt and remove from the heat. Serve hot as is, or purée to your desired texture using a stick blender.

SERVES 6–8

120ml extra virgin olive oil
2 white onions, diced
3 garlic cloves, finely chopped
2 tablespoons ground coriander
1 tablespoon ground cumin
½ teaspoon freshly ground black pepper
2 large carrots, peeled and diced
750g small red lentils, picked over
juice of 1 lemon
1 tablespoon sea salt

HARIRA

Harira was the soup of kings in Morocco during the Ramadan holidays. It was always offered in a covered pot, into which an egg would be cracked while the king looked on. If the soup was hot enough to poach the egg, then it was heated to his liking. This traditional soup requires some time and patience, but it's worth preparing an extra-large batch because it gets better over the course of a few days. The exact translation of harira is 'silky' – an apt description.

COOKING TIP Make sure the soup is very hot before you crack the egg into it; the white and yolk should firm up within a minute or two. Harira will keep, covered and refrigerated, for up to 1 week, or in resealable bags in the freezer, for up to 2 months.

Combine the allspice, 1 tablespoon salt, pepper, turmeric, nutmeg, saffron and cardamom in a small bowl. Place the meat in a large bowl, pour half the spice mixture on top and, using your hands, toss the spices and meat together to coat it all over.

In a large stockpot, heat the oil over a high heat. Add the meat and brown all over, turning occasionally, then tip in the shallots and sauté until soft and fragrant, about 3 minutes. Stir in the garlic and cook until golden and fragrant, about 30 seconds, then the tomato purée; coating the meat and vegetables and sautéing for 3–5 minutes. Add the fresh tomatoes and cook until they release their juices, about 5 minutes, then the carrots and celery and sauté until softened, about 3 minutes. Scatter over the coriander, parsley and the remaining spice mixture and cook until fragrant, 1–2 minutes. Pour in 8 litres water and bring to the boil for 3–5 minutes, then reduce the heat to low, add the remaining 1 tablespoon salt, lentils and chickpeas, bay leaves, cloves and cinnamon sticks, cover and cook until the meat falls apart, 1½–2 hours, stirring occasionally. Stir in the vermicelli during the last 5 minutes of cooking.

Meanwhile, carefully crack the egg, if using, into a small bowl – do not break the yolk – and squeeze the lemon juice over it. Remove the pan from the heat and slide the egg into the soup; the egg should set quickly. Serve immediately.

SERVES 8–10

1 tablespoon ground allspice
2 tablespoons sea salt, or to taste
1 teaspoon freshly ground black pepper
1 teaspoon turmeric
¾ teaspoon ground nutmeg
½ teaspoon saffron threads
½ teaspoon ground cardamom
1kg lamb shoulder, cut into 4cm pieces, or one 1kg chicken, cut into eighths
80ml extra-virgin olive or vegetable oil
4 shallots, chopped
3 garlic cloves, chopped
2 tablespoons tomato purée
4 plum tomatoes, chopped
2 carrots, peeled and chopped
2 celery sticks, diced
60g chopped fresh coriander
30g chopped fresh flat-leaf parsley
150g brown lentils
100g red lentils
1 (400g) tin chickpeas, drained
3 bay leaves
3 whole cloves
2 cinnamon sticks
200g broken vermicelli
1 medium egg (optional)
juice of 1 lemon (optional)

PURÉED SPLIT PEA SOUP

SHORABIT BAZZELA

**This beautiful hearty soup makes a great vegetarian meal. I prefer using
dried green split peas rather than the yellow variety, which customers at the
restaurant often mistake for lentils. Of course, you can substitute any colour –
yellow, orange or brown – and it won't noticeably change the taste. If you want
more intense flavour, stir in some garlicky *Teklai* (page 196) at the very end.
I serve this soup with toasted Za'atar Bread (page 58) and Homemade Hot Sauce
(page 194).**

Place 200ml oil in a large stockpot over a medium heat and sauté the onions until soft
and fragrant, about 3 minutes. Add the shallots and sauté for a further 3 minutes. Stir in
the garlic and cook until fragrant, about 3–5 minutes. Mix in the coriander, cumin, salt
and pepper and heat until fragrant, about 30 seconds, then the coriander, cooking for
2–3 minutes. Add the carrots and cook until softened, about 3 minutes, then the spinach,
if using, until it begins to wilt. Add the split peas and 1.25–1.75 litres water and bring to
the boil. Reduce the heat, cover and simmer for 30 minutes.

Remove the soup from the heat and drizzle with the remaining olive oil. Purée using
a stick blender, then ladle into bowls, add a dollop of *teklai*, if using, and garnish with
the parsley. Serve with the za'atar bread, hot sauce and lemon wedges.

VARIATION *Teklai is a wonderful flavouring, but herbed teklai takes it right over the
top: simply sauté 30g chopped fresh coriander and 1 chopped chilli after cooking the
garlic in basic teklai.*

SERVES 6–8

250ml olive oil

100g chopped white onions

2 shallots, chopped

8 garlic cloves, finely chopped (about
  2 tablespoons)

2 tablespoons ground coriander

½ tablespoon ground cumin

½ teaspoon sea salt, or to taste

½ tablespoon freshly ground black pepper

80g chopped fresh coriander

100g peeled and chopped carrots

40g chopped spinach (optional)

440g dried green split peas, picked over

1 tablespoon *Teklai* (page 196; optional)

30g chopped fresh flat-leaf parsley,
  for garnish

Za'atar Bread (page 58), Homemade
  Hot Sauce (page 194) and lemon
  wedges, for serving

SIMPLE CHICKEN SOUP

---•◆•---

SHORABIT DJAJ

Every cook needs a restorative chicken soup in their repertoire. This Palestinian version is typically made when preparing the Seasoned Chicken with Stock (below). If you have the stock to hand, it can be made in a matter of minutes – there's no sautéing vegetables or simmering necessary. My grown-up kids still request this soup, whether they're under the weather or not. Serve with warm Arabic bread.

Bring the stock to the boil in a large saucepan over a high heat. Add the vermicelli or rice, reduce the heat, cover and cook until the noodles are al dente or the rice is tender but not mushy.

Ladle the soup into bowls, squeeze some lemon over each and garnish with parsley.

SERVES 6–8

2.5 litres stock from Seasoned Chicken
    with Stock (see below)
150g vermicelli or 75g Egyptian rice
lemon wedges, for squeezing
chopped fresh flat-leaf parsley, for garnish

SEASONED CHICKEN WITH STOCK

In a small bowl, combine the allspice, salt, pepper, cardamom and nutmeg. Rub half this spice mixture all over the chicken pieces and set the remaining mixture aside.

In a large stockpot, heat the oil over a medium-high heat. Working in batches if necessary, sear the chickens all over, about 3 minutes per side. Add the cinnamon stick, onion, bay leaves, cloves and 3.75–5 litres water. Bring to the boil for 5 minutes, skimming the surface with a spoon, then add the remaining spice mixture, reduce the heat and simmer, partially covered, for 1 hour.

Transfer the chickens to a plate with a slotted spoon. Remove the meat from the bone and use as desired.

Allow the stock to cool, then store in resealable freezer bags for up to 2 months.

MAKES 5–6 LITRES STOCK
AND 3KG MEAT

2 tablespoons ground allspice
1 tablespoon sea salt
1 tablespoon freshly ground black pepper
½ teaspoon ground cardamom
½ teaspoon ground nutmeg
2 chickens (1–1.5kg each), cut into
    6–8 pieces each, washed and patted dry
120ml extra virgin olive oil or vegetable oil
1 cinnamon stick
1 white onion, halved
5 bay leaves
5 whole cloves

COOLING STOCK It is essential to bring the temperature of stock down quickly to avoid the risk of bacterial growth. To cool quickly, place the bowl or pot, uncovered, into a cold-water bath, ideally a sink full of ice water. Stir the stock often. Once it's cooled to lukewarm, pour into resealable freezer bags and freeze for up to 2 months.

✦ OLIVES, LEMONS & ZA'ATAR ✦

SMOKED WHEAT BERRY SOUP

SHORABIT FREEKAH

My mother always made this soup with turkey necks because she believed they had a different flavour than whole chickens. My version, made with seasoned poached chicken and stock, is every bit as delicious – and very simple to prepare. I used to make this for my kids a lot; if you have the stock prepared, all it requires is quickly sautéing some shallots and combining a few ingredients in a pot.

Look for freekeh (smoked and cracked green wheat berries) that is chopped into very fine pieces; if you can't find it, put the larger-grained version in the food processor and pulse until it has the consistency of coarse grain. Serve this soup with toasted Arabic bread.

Place the oil in a large stockpot over a medium-high heat and sauté the shallots until soft and fragrant, about 3 minutes. Add 2.5 litres stock, the parts of 1 whole chicken or half of the lamb and the freekeh and bring to the boil. Cook for 10 minutes, then reduce the heat, cover and simmer until the freekeh is done to the desired consistency, about 30 minutes.

Ladle the soup into bowls, garnish with the parsley and serve hot, with the lemon wedges on the side.

VARIATION *To make this the way my mother did, substitute turkey necks for the chicken, about 2kg in total, when preparing the stock. Put one cooked neck in each bowl of soup and serve.*

SERVES 6–10

60ml vegetable oil
2 shallots, chopped
Seasoned Chicken with Stock (see opposite) or Seasoned Lamb with Stock (page 102)
100g fine-grained freekeh (roasted and cracked green wheat berries)
4 teaspoons chopped fresh flat-leaf parsley
lemon wedges, for serving

LAMB AND VEGETABLE SOUP

SHORABAT KHOUDRAH

My mother loved making hearty vegetable soups and always used more vegetables than we could count! She happily mixed root vegetables with the classic trio of squash, tomatoes and celery, and of course, she chopped her vegetables into small, perfect squares. I suspect chopping was a form of meditation for her. I, however, am a bit looser in my methodology (and I won't hold you to including all of the vegetables in the ingredients list), but I still prepare this soup the day before I want to serve it, the way my mother did. She insisted it was better the second day. It most certainly is.

⚜ **COOKING TIP** Of course, you can omit the lamb and use vegetable stock instead of lamb stock to make a vegetarian version.

Place the oil in large stockpot over a medium heat and sauté the shallots until golden brown, 5–8 minutes. Stir in the cardamom and pepper until fragrant, about 30 seconds, then add the celery, potatoes and carrots and cook until the vegetables begin to soften, 5–8 minutes.

Tip in the courgette, sweetcorn and artichoke hearts and sauté for a further 5 minutes. Add the tomatoes and coriander and cook, stirring, for 2 minutes to soften the tomatoes.

Cut 500g lamb meat into 1.2cm pieces and add this and 2.5–3 litres of the stock to the pan. Season with salt and bring to the boil, then reduce the heat, cover and simmer for 5 minutes. Serve hot.

SERVES 6

2 tablespoons extra virgin olive oil
100g chopped shallots or white onion
½ teaspoon ground cardamom
½ teaspoon freshly ground black pepper
4 celery sticks, chopped
2 white potatoes, peeled and
    coarsely chopped
2 carrots, peeled and coarsely chopped
4 baby courgettes, coarsely chopped or cut
    into 1.2cm-thick half moons
100–150g fresh sweetcorn kernels
    (from 2 cobs)
7 fresh or frozen artichoke hearts, chopped
2 plum tomatoes, chopped
30g chopped coriander (optional)
Seasoned Lamb with Stock (page 102)
sea salt, to taste

SEAFOOD SOUP

— ·◆· —

SHORABIT AKL BAHRI

I created this soup for my son, Tarek, who loves seafood above all else. There's nothing quite like the flavour of the very freshest fish and shellfish cooked in a herbed stock; I use as many fresh, fragrant herbs as I can get my hands on. Of course, it's okay to substitute more of one for another, but the combination of fresh coriander, basil, dill and oregano is ideal. It is unusual to find cumin in a seafood soup, but I find a touch subtly warms the stock. The beauty of this soup is in its versatility: you can use whatever firm fish you like. Sometimes I prepare it with root vegetables, other times, I add more chopped tomatoes to make the soup resemble a classic bouillabaisse. The recipe can be halved, if you like.

Combine the salt, pepper and cumin, if using, in a small bowl. Sprinkle a third of the seasoning mixture over the snapper and set the remaining two-thirds aside.

Place the oil in a large stockpot over a medium heat and sauté the fish, turning once, until golden brown, 3–4 minutes per side. Using a fish spatula, transfer the fish to a kitchen-paper–lined platter.

Add the prawns and calamari to the same pot and cook, stirring occasionally, 3–5 minutes. Using the fish spatula, transfer the calamari and prawns to the kitchen paper–lined platter.

Add the shallots to the same pot and cook until soft and fragrant, about 5 minutes. Tip in the potatoes, carrots and celery, and cook, stirring once or twice, for a further 5 minutes. Stir in the coriander, basil, dill and oregano, until fragrant, about 3 minutes. Pour in the stock or water and bring to the boil. Reduce the heat, add the bay leaves, cover and simmer until the vegetables are soft and the stock thickens slightly, 15–20 minutes.

In the meantime, debone the fish and add it, along with the reserved prawns and calamari, sage leaf and tomatoes, to the pot; cook for a further 5 minutes. For a more intense flavour, add the fish head. Remove from the heat, take out the sage leaf and the bay leaves and stir in the lemon juice. Ladle into soup bowls and garnish with chopped parsley.

SERVES 10

1 tablespoon sea salt

1½ teaspoons freshly ground black pepper

1½ teaspoons ground cumin (optional)

250ml extra virgin olive oil

1 whole red snapper (about 500g)

10 medium prawns, peeled, deveined and cut into 5–7.5cm pieces

225g calamari, cut into thin rings

3 shallots, chopped

2 baking potatoes, peeled and diced

2 medium carrots, peeled and diced

2 sticks of celery, diced

30g chopped fresh coriander

30g chopped fresh basil

1 tablespoon chopped fresh dill

1 tablespoon chopped fresh oregano

4 litres chicken stock or water

3 bay leaves

1 fresh sage leaf

4 plum tomatoes, chopped

juice of 1 lemon

2 tablespoons chopped fresh flat-leaf parsley, for garnish

CAULIFLOWER AND LAMB STEW

YAKHNIT ZAHRA

When I was eighteen, I taught fifth-grade students in Haifa. At the weekend, I would return home to Nazareth, where this soothing stew routinely awaited me. My mother knew it was a favourite of mine – and it still is. I've added my own flourishes to intensify its flavour: the fresh coriander and pomegranate molasses are transformative. This recipe is perfect for vegetarians, as it doesn't rely on the meat for its flavour; simply use vegetable stock, omit the meat and enjoy it just the same, ladled over fragrant basmati rice.

COOKING TIP If you are preparing this in advance, keep the meat and cauliflower separate until just before you plan to heat and serve the stew.

Place the vegetable oil in a high-sided frying pan over a high heat and fry the cauliflower in batches, turning occasionally, until it is golden brown all over. Using a slotted spoon, transfer the cauliflower to a kitchen-paper-lined platter and set aside. Alternatively, preheat the oven to 250°C/gas mark 9. Arrange the cauliflower florets on a baking sheet and brush all over with 120ml olive oil. Roast until deep golden, about 25 minutes. Set aside.

In a small bowl, combine the allspice, salt, pepper, cumin and nutmeg. In a large casserole dish, heat 60ml olive oil over a medium-high heat. Add the garlic and sauté until soft and golden, 3–5 minutes. Stir in the spice mixture until fragrant, about 30 seconds, then the coriander. Pour in 1.75 litres stock and the lemon juice and bring to the boil, then stir in 30g *teklai* – it will make a wonderful swishing sound. Add the pomegranate molasses, if using, then the lamb with the cauliflower and stir to combine. Bring to the boil, then reduce the heat and simmer for 10 minutes.

Ladle into soup bowls and serve with the remaining *teklai* on the side, along with either of the rice options.

VARIATION *Add the juice of 1 lemon to the remaining* teklai *to make a delicious sauce for spooning over the stew and rice.*

SERVES 6–8

500ml vegetable oil

3 large or 4 small heads cauliflower, cored and cut into large florets

1 tablespoon ground allspice

1½ teaspoons sea salt

1 teaspoon freshly ground black pepper

1 teaspoon ground cumin

⅓ teaspoon ground nutmeg

60ml extra virgin olive oil

5 garlic cloves, crushed

80g chopped fresh coriander

Seasoned Lamb with Stock (page 102)

juice of 1½ lemons, or to taste

Teklai (page 196)

3 tablespoons pomegranate molasses, or to taste (optional)

Basmati Vegetable Rice (page 183) or Rice and Vermicelli Pilaf (page 182)

CHOPPED MLOOKHIA STEW

— ◆ —

MLOOKHIA NAAMEH

Literally translated, *mlookhia* means 'the food of kings' because at one time, the spinach-like leaf, a member of the jute family, required very special attention to grow and to prepare, thus making it available only to the wealthy. These days, everyone in the Middle East eats the earthy, herbaceous green, which boasts a higher iron content than spinach. Fresh green *mlookhia* is nearly non-existent in Europe. The frozen greens are more readily available, so I call for them along with the dried version, both of which are widely available at specialist shops and Middle Eastern markets.

    The preparation of this stew varies from one country to another – in Lebanon and Syria, it is topped with chopped raw onion, red or white wine vinegar and toasted Arabic bread, as it is here. Egyptians stir in garlicky *Teklai* (page 196) and squeeze a bit of lemon juice into the stew just before serving. I like to serve it with Rice and Vermicelli Pilaf (page 182).

Preheat the oven to 230°C/gas mark 8.

Place the oil in a large casserole dish over a medium heat and sauté the onion until fragrant, about 3 minutes. Stir in the tomato, salt, pepper and nutmeg and cook for a further 3 minutes. Pour in 2.75 litres of the stock and bring to the boil. Add the dried *mlookhia* and return the stew to the boil, stirring occasionally, for a further 5 minutes. Tip in the frozen *mlookhia* and return to the boil – a thick white foam will appear on the top. Using a large spoon, skim off the foam from the surface until it no longer appears. Stir 3 tablespoons *teklai* into the boiling stew – it should make a sizzling sound as it hits the hot stock. Remove from the heat.

In a medium bowl, combine the lemon juice, ghee and remaining 250ml chicken stock and 1 tablespoon *teklai*. Arrange the seasoned chicken pieces in a large baking dish, drizzle over the lemony broth and roast, uncovered, until the chicken is slightly crispy on top, about 30 minutes. Set aside to cool. When cool enough to handle, remove the chicken from the bone.

To serve, divide the toasted Arabic bread among individual soup bowls, top with the rice pilaf, then ladle the *mlookhia* over it all. Top each serving with chicken and 2–3 tablespoons of diced onion. Serve the vinegar on the side.

SERVES 6–8

6 tablespoons vegetable oil
1 small white onion, finely chopped
1 plum tomato, finely chopped
½ teaspoon sea salt
½ teaspoon freshly ground black pepper
¼ teaspoon ground nutmeg
3 litres stock from Seasoned Chicken
    with Stock (page 90) or chicken stock
50g chopped dried *mlookhia*
4 (400g) bags frozen chopped *mlookhia*
30g *Teklai* (page 196)
juice of 3 lemons
30g ghee or butter
Arabic bread (page 57), toasted
Rice and Vermicelli Pilaf (page 182)
1 large white onion, diced
red or white wine vinegar, for serving

GARLICKY BEAN AND TOMATO STEW

FASOOLYA KHADRA

I prefer making this very basic stew with fresh runner beans. Obviously, fresh produce always tastes better, but if you are in a pinch, frozen vegetables make a fine substitute. I do draw the line at tinned vegetables – always mushy, never good. This recipe can be a staple on your weekday menu – when beans are in season, you can use any variety. And, as with most Middle Eastern soups, this one is even better the next day! Serve with Arabic Bread (page 57) and Rice and Vermicelli Pilaf (page 182).

Place the oil in a large casserole dish over a high heat for 30 seconds. When hot but not smoking, add the shallots and sauté until soft and fragrant, about 3 minutes, then stir in the garlic until golden, a further 3 minutes.

In a small dish, combine the coriander, allspice and black pepper. Stir the spice mixture into the pot and heat until fragrant. Add the runner beans and salt and stir to incorporate. Reduce the heat to medium, cover and cook for 10 minutes or until the beans are tender. Stir in the plum tomatoes, cover and cook until the tomatoes begin to soften, 4–5 minutes. Add the chopped tomatoes and lemon juice and cook for a further 3–5 minutes, then stir in the *teklai*, add the chilli, if using, and serve hot.

VARIATION *To make this a beef or lamb stew, prepare Seasoned Beef or Lamb with Stock (page 102). Add 500ml of the beef or lamb stock plus the boiled meat to the pot after adding the lemon juice. Raise the heat to high, cover and bring to the boil; cook 3 minutes. Uncover and cook for a further 15 minutes to allow the mixture to thicken slightly. Stir in the teklai and chilli, if using. Remove from the heat.*

SERVES 8–10

250ml extra virgin olive oil

2 shallots, diced

10 garlic cloves, finely chopped

2 heaped tablespoons ground coriander

1 teaspoon–½ tablespoon allspice

1 teaspoon freshly ground black pepper

2.5kg runner beans, both ends trimmed and cut into 4cm pieces

1 tablespoon sea salt, or to taste

6 plum tomatoes, chopped, with their juices

1 (400g) tin chopped tomatoes

juice of ½ lemon or 3 tablespoons lemon juice

1 tablespoon *Teklai* (page 196)

1 chilli, finely diced (optional)

SPINACH STEW WITH BEEF OR LAMB

— ◆ —

YAKHNIT SABANIKH

In the past, Palestinian cooks were more likely to cook this iron-rich, healthy stew when spinach was abundant in their gardens, but now that spinach is available throughout the year, it is made whenever the desire strikes. Pickled Jalapeños and Carrots (page 189) make a delicious accompaniment. Serve with Rice and Vermicelli Pilaf (page 182) or with Arabic Bread (page 57).

Place the oil in a large casserole dish over a high heat and sauté the garlic until golden brown, 2–3 minutes. Stir in the coriander and pepper until fragrant, about 1 minute, then the spinach, cooking until it wilts, 2–3 minutes. Add the boiled meat, 1.5 litres stock and the split peas; increase the heat and bring to the boil for 5 minutes, then reduce the heat and simmer for 10 minutes.

Ladle into bowls and drizzle each serving with the lemon juice and, if desired, the pomegranate molasses.

SERVES 6–8

120ml extra virgin olive oil
10 garlic cloves, finely chopped
2 tablespoons ground coriander
1½ teaspoons freshly ground black pepper
1.5kg fresh baby spinach, roughly chopped
Seasoned Lamb or Beef with Stock
　(page 102)
220g split peas, boiled for 10 minutes
　and drained
juice of 2 lemons
2 tablespoons pomegranate molasses
　(optional)

SEASONED LAMB OR BEEF WITH STOCK

In a small bowl, combine the allspice, salt, pepper and nutmeg. Place the lamb or beef in a medium bowl and tip over half of the spice mixture. Using your hands, rub the spice mixture into the meat, coating all sides thoroughly. Set the remaining spice mixture aside.

Place the oil in a large casserole dish over a high heat. When hot, sear the meat on all sides, about 3 minutes. Add the cardamom, bay leaves, cloves, cinnamon stick, onion, the remaining spice mixture and enough water to cover by 7.5cm. Bring to the boil for 5 minutes, then reduce the heat to medium-low and simmer, skimming the fat from the surface with a slotted spoon, for 40–60 minutes for lamb and 60–90 minutes for beef, or until the meat is fork tender. Strain the stock into a bowl, allow to cool and use the meat as desired or place in resealable plastic bags and refrigerate for up to 3 days or freeze up to 2 months.

MAKES 5–6 LITRES STOCK AND 1.5KG MEAT

1 tablespoon ground allspice
1 tablespoon sea salt
1½ teaspoons freshly ground black pepper
1 cinnamon stick, halved lengthways,
　or ⅓ teaspoon ground cinnamon
⅓ teaspoon ground nutmeg
1.5kg lamb meat from the leg or beef
　sirloin, cut into 4cm cubes
120ml vegetable oil
5 whole cardamom pods
3 bay leaves
2 whole cloves
1 white onion, cut in half

COOLING STOCK It is essential to bring the temperature of stock down quickly to avoid the risk of bacterial growth. To cool quickly, place the bowl or pot, uncovered, into a cold-water bath, ideally a sink full of ice water. Stir the stock often. Once it's cooled to lukewarm, pour into resealable freezer bags and freeze for up to 2 months.

SWEET PEA AND KAFTA STEW

— ◆ —

YAKHNIT BAZELLA BELKAFTA

Most Palestinian cooks make this with cubes of lamb and serve it with rice, but my mother made it with kafta (minced lamb mixed with parsley and onion and shaped into small kebabs) and served it with mashed potatoes. When tender sugarsnap peas are in season, I use them in place of the frozen sweet peas. If you don't want to use kafta here, add the lamb or beef from the Seasoned Stock with Lamb or Beef (page 102), during the last 5 minutes of simmering.

Shape the kafta into 4cm x 2.5cm fingers. Place the oil in a large casserole dish over a medium heat and, working in batches if necessary, lightly sear the kafta until golden brown, turning once, about 3–4 minutes in total. Using a slotted spatula, transfer the kafta to a kitchen paper–lined platter to drain.

Using the same dish, sauté the shallots and garlic until lightly browned, 3–4 minutes. Stir in the coriander, allspice, salt, black pepper and nutmeg until fragrant, about 2 minutes, then reduce the heat, add the peas and carrots and cook until just softened, about 5 minutes. Add the fresh and chopped tinned tomatoes and the stock. Raise the heat, bring to the boil, then reduce the heat and simmer for 15–20 minutes. Add the reserved kafta fingers and simmer for a further 5 minutes. Serve hot.

SERVES 8

Kafta (page 158)
120ml vegetable oil
3 shallots, diced
8 garlic cloves, crushed or finely chopped
1 tablespoon ground coriander
1 teaspoon ground allspice
1 tablespoon sea salt
½ tablespoon freshly ground black pepper
⅓ teaspoon ground nutmeg
⅓ teaspoon cardamom (optional)
4 (400g) bags frozen petits pois
2 carrots, peeled and diced
4 fresh plum tomatoes, chopped (optional)
2 (400g) tins chopped tomatoes
1 litre stock from Seasoned Lamb or Beef with Stock (page 102) or beef stock or water

RED LENTIL AND BUTTERNUT SQUASH STEW

— ◆ —

If you make this stew once, there is no going back. The butternut squash adds a mellow sweetness but it is also delicious with chunks of yams, carrots or even pumpkin. Use one of these vegetables or a mix to make this stew, and serve it piping hot, warm (my preference), or chilled.

Heat 6 tablespoons olive oil in a large casserole dish over medium-high heat. When hot, sauté the shallots and onion until soft and golden, 3–4 minutes. Stir in the garlic until fragrant, about 30 seconds, then the chillies, coriander, cumin, black pepper, about 1 minute. Add the squash and stir to incorporate, then reduce the heat and cook, covered, about 10 minutes.

Tip in the lentils and 1 litre water, then cover and cook for about 12 minutes. If the squash has not softened, add 250ml additional water, cover and cook for a further 10 minutes.

Ladle the stew into serving bowls, drizzle with olive oil and serve.

SERVES 6–8

120ml olive oil, plus extra for drizzling
4 shallots, chopped
1 onion, chopped
8 garlic cloves, crushed
2 chillies, such as jalapeños or poblanos
a large handful of chopped fresh coriander
2 tablespoons ground coriander
1 tablespoon ground cumin
1 tablespoon freshly ground black pepper
2 butternut squash, peeled and diced
340g red lentils, picked over

WHITE BEAN AND BEEF STEW

· ◆ ·

YAKHNIT FASOOLYA BAIDA

As a child, I remember watching some of my schoolmates bite into whole raw garlic cloves or onions in between spoonfuls of this extra-hearty stew. Popular throughout the Levant, this rather old recipe was commonly prepared in winter, when fresh vegetables were spare and beans were in every pantry. It is invariably served with olives and pickles to add salty, briny flavour. Serve with Rice and Vermicelli Pilaf (page 182) or Basmati Vegetable Rice (page 183).

Place the oil in a large casserole dish over a medium heat and sauté the shallots until golden brown, about 3 minutes. Stir in the garlic until fragrant, then the chillies, coriander, cumin, black pepper and allspice, about 30 seconds. Add the celery and carrots and cook until the vegetables soften, stirring frequently, about 5 minutes. Add the coriander and sauté to mellow its flavour, about 2 minutes. Add the plum tomatoes and stir until the tomatoes release some of their juices, 2–3 minutes. Add the tomato purée and chilli paste and stir continuously for a further 3 minutes.

Add 1–1.5kg of the meat with 1.5 litres of the stock and the chopped tomatoes. Bring to the boil. Add the beans and sugar. Return to the boil until the liquid thickens slightly, 10–15 minutes. Stir in the hot *teklai* and listen for the swoosh. Remove from the heat and serve.

VEGETARIAN VARIATION In Nazareth, white beans and beef always went together; you never served the beans without the meat. But once I opened my restaurant, I learned from some of my staff that beans themselves can carry a dish, particularly when a mix of spices and the *teklai* are added to the pot. To make the vegetarian version of this stew, simply omit the meat and use vegetable stock in place of the meat stock.

SERVES 8–10

250ml olive oil

3 shallots, diced

2 tablespoons finely chopped garlic

2 long green or jalapeño chillies, deseeded and finely chopped (seeds reserved if desired)

1½ tablespoons ground coriander

1 tablespoon ground cumin

1 tablespoon freshly ground black pepper

1 tablespoon ground allspice

2 sticks of celery, diced

2 small carrots, peeled and diced

60g chopped fresh coriander

4 plum tomatoes, diced

3 tablespoons tomato purée

1 tablespoon seedless Middle Eastern or Turkish chilli paste

Seasoned Lamb or Beef with Stock (page 102)

2 (400g) tins chopped tomatoes

1kg small dried white beans, soaked (page 21) and boiled or 6 (400g) tins cannellini beans, drained and rinsed

1 teaspoon sugar or ½ teaspoon lemon salt

3 tablespoons *Teklai* (page 196)

Rice and Vermicelli Pilaf (page 182) or Basmati Vegetable Rice (page 183), for serving

BEEF AND POTATO STEW

— ◆ —

YAKHNIT BATATA

It is a rare Palestinian storecupboad that doesn't have a basket filled with potatoes in it. They are used in so many traditional Middle Eastern dishes, including this 'peasant' stew, a combination of beef and potatoes seasoned with allspice, coriander, nutmeg and cardamom. I prefer using beef sirloin in this recipe, but you could use a less expensive cut and allow the soup to simmer until the meat is fork-tender.

Place the oil in a large casserole dish over a medium heat and sauté the onion until golden brown, 4–5 minutes. Stir in the garlic, chilli, allspice, pepper, coriander, cumin, nutmeg and cardamom until fragrant, about 1 minute. Tip in the carrots and the beef and cook, stirring, until the beef is seared on all sides. Add the tomatoes, fresh coriander and the beef stock and stir with a wooden spoon, scraping up the crispy bits from the bottom of the pot. Cover and leave to simmer until the meat is tender, 60–90 minutes.

Meanwhile, in a large, deep frying pan, heat 500ml vegetable oil over medium-high heat. Working in batches if necessary, fry the potatoes, turning occasionally, until they are golden brown all over. Using a slotted spoon, transfer to a paper-towel lined plate and set aside. The potatoes can be made one day in advance and stored in a container with a tight-fitting lid in the refrigerator. Alternatively, brush the potatoes liberally with the oil and arrange in a single layer on a baking sheet or in a roasting pan. Roast in a 175°F/gas mark 4 oven until golden and crispy, about 30 minutes. Repeat this same step with the onions and an extra 500ml vegetable oil, if roasting.

Uncover the casserole dish and add the potatoes, pearl onions and lemon juice and season with salt. Simmer for 5 minutes before serving hot.

VARIATION Chicken may be substituted for the beef: use 1 whole chicken cut into 8 pieces or 1kg boneless chicken breasts cut into 2.5–5cm cubes. Season with salt and pepper, then sear on all sides in a frying pan slicked with olive oil over a medium-high heat.

VARIATION If you can find tamarind paste, use it in place of the lemon juice. Soak 225g tamarind paste in 500ml boiling water and let it dissolve. Pass the liquid through a sieve and use in the same proportion as the lemon juice. The tamarind liquid will keep, tightly covered, in the fridge for up to 2 weeks. Alternatively, substitute shop-bought liquid tamarind for the lemon juice.

SERVES 6–8

120ml olive oil

1 red onion, chopped

10 garlic cloves, crushed

2 chillies, deseeded and finely chopped

1 tablespoon ground allspice

1 tablespoon freshly ground black pepper

1 tablespoon ground coriander

½ tablespoon ground cumin

⅓ teaspoon ground nutmeg (optional)

⅓ teaspoon ground cardamom (optional)

2 carrots, peeled and diced or thinly sliced

1kg beef sirloin, cut into 5cm cubes

2 plum tomatoes, chopped

1 bunch fresh coriander, chopped

2.75 litres beef stock or water

500ml–1 litre vegetable oil

6 baking potatoes, peeled, each chopped into 8–10 pieces and fried or roasted

500g silverskin onions, peeled and fried or roasted

120ml fresh lemon juice

sea salt, to taste

OKRA STEW WITH LAMB AND POMEGRANATE MOLASSES

YAKHNIT BAMYA

When I first found okra in the markets in the US, I was dumbstruck by its size. In fact, I brought it home and, like any good Middle Eastern cook, I tried to stuff it! Okra is traditionally cooked with tomato (page 180), but my mum always made hers with lemon juice and pomegranate molasses – her way of working around the exorbitant number of tomato-based dishes in Middle Eastern cuisine. Of course, I couldn't leave well enough alone, so I added coriander and chilli to her recipe. I love the assertive seasonings in this stew; the sweet yet sour pomegranate molasses and the herby coriander pair well with the rich flavours of the lamb and okra. Serve this stew with Rice and Vermicelli Pilaf (page 182), or scoop it up with warm Arabic Bread (page 57).

❖ COOKING TIP I find fresh okra generally too big to use in this stew – it is filled with seeds and produce an unappealing texture when cooked – but if you find it in diminutive form, then by all means use it. Be sure to cut the stems away first.

Place 120ml oil in a frying pan over medium-high heat and, working in batches, fry the okra, turning so that it takes on colour all over, 6–8 minutes. Using a slotted spoon, transfer to a paper towel–lined plate. Alternatively, pat dry the okra and arrange in a single layer on a baking tray or in a roasting pan. Brush liberally with the oil and roast in a 240°F/gas mark 8 oven until light golden.

Place 120ml oil in a large casserole dish over a medium heat and sauté the garlic until golden brown, about 3 minutes. Stir in the coriander until fragrant, about 30 seconds, then the allspice, black pepper, cumin, nutmeg and 2.5 litres lamb stock; bring to the boil. Add the fried okra and lamb, season with salt and continue to cook until the okra softens, about 10 minutes. Stir in the pomegranate molasses and simmer for a further 2 minutes. Remove from the heat and squeeze in the lemon juice. Serve with the rice pilaf and hot peppers.

SERVES 8

120ml plus 120ml extra virgin olive oil
6 (500g) bags frozen baby okra, rinsed and thoroughly drained, fried or roasted (page 180)
3 tablespoons finely chopped garlic
2 tablespoons ground coriander
1 tablespoon ground allspice
1 teaspoon freshly ground black pepper
½ teaspoon ground cumin
½ teaspoon ground nutmeg
Seasoned Lamb with Stock (page 102)
sea salt, to taste
60ml pomegranate molasses
juice of 1 large lemon
Rice and Vermicelli Pilaf (page 182)
hot chillies, for serving

MAIN COURSES

BIG DISHES

The idea of eating the biggest meal of the day at dinnertime was foreign to me until I moved to New York. Back home in Nazareth, lunch, or *ghada*, was the grand meal and it was always served in the late afternoon. In the evening, we generally ate a variation of breakfast. Admittedly, there are times when I still like to eat this way, but after 30 years of living in the States, I've made the transition!

In this chapter, there is a wonderful mix of classic Middle Eastern dishes and others of my own invention. Many are straightforward, simple recipes that can be prepared for weeknight dinners – Prawns in Garlic Sauce (page 130) and *Mhammar* (page 144), the classic chicken and potato dish, and *Shakshuka* (page 115), a comforting combination of seasoned tomato sauce and eggs, also known as Eggs in Purgatory. Others are meant to be prepared for special occasions and celebrations or on a leisurely Sunday when the day revolves around preparing a big meal. The traditional dishes are here – *Mansaaf* (page 157), a classic combination of Egyptian rice, lamb and pine nuts; *Sayadiyya* (page 125), the fisherman's dish; and both chicken and fish tagines (page 145 and page 126 respectively) along with a handful of Tanoreen specialities in which I have tinkered with tradition – Aubergine Napoleon (page 119) and Tanoreen Baked Fish (page 121) among them. In fact, my customers are increasingly looking for meatless main courses, to which I have responded by modifying several traditional Middle Eastern recipes into *styami*, or vegetarian-style meals. I've included them here because to my mind, they've earned their place in the Tanoreen repertoire.

As you flip through these pages, you will notice that I am not shy when it comes to using warm, fragrant spices in my cooking, particularly when I am making a slow-cooked dish. I reach for smoky cumin, sweet cinnamon and earthy allspice almost reflexively when I step into the kitchen. After years of seasoning my dishes with one spice at a time, I created a custom blend for using at the restaurant. In the dishes that follow, I offer as close to those measurements as possible. Fresh herbs, too, are an essential part of my generously seasoned dishes. Basil, coriander and parsley all brighten the flavour of a warmly scented dish and also add a wonderfully herbaceous green note. At Tanoreen, I am quite heavy-handed with the parsley (a source of endless teasing by my daughter Jumana) because I like my platters to look like a garden. You will also notice that I cook primarily with olive oil. Traditionally, all dishes featuring meat are prepared with ghee or butter, but I do as my mother did. How could she not? She grew up in an olive-growing family!

The following pages are filled with what I call big dishes – big flavours, generous servings and storied origins. I like to think of it as the chapter in which you will spend time reading the recipes, enjoying the stories, and cooking and eating with people you truly care about. That's what I do – every day – and I can't think of a more pleasurable way to spend my time.

'BACK HOME IN NAZARETH, LUNCH, OR *GHADA*, WAS THE GRAND MEAL AND IT WAS ALWAYS SERVED IN THE LATE AFTERNOON. IN THE EVENING, WE GENERALLY ATE A VARIATION OF BREAKFAST. ADMITTEDLY, THERE ARE TIMES WHEN I STILL LIKE TO EAT THIS WAY, BUT AFTER 30 YEARS OF LIVING IN THE STATES, I'VE MADE THE TRANSITION!'

BAKED AUBERGINE

◦•◦

SINIYAT EL FOKRRA

Siniyat el fokrra, **which means 'a tray for the poor', is this dish's name because it makes use of whatever leftover vegetables are in the house. My mother's preparation didn't feature herbs or nuts, which were unaffordable for home cooks at the time. I thought it needed a bit of brightening and some crunch, so I sprinkled both in. It is a forgiving dish; use aubergine entirely if you don't have or like squash. Serve with pickles and sliced chillies.**

⚜ **COOKING TIP** Leftover baked aubergine freezes beautifully. Cut it into individual servings, wrap well and freeze for up to 2 months. Simply defrost and reheat in a 175°C/gas mark 4 oven.

Heat 60ml oil in a large frying pan over a medium-high heat and sauté the onions until amber, 7–8 minutes. Stir in the garlic until fragrant, 1–2 minutes, then the allspice, coriander, pepper, cumin and paprika, if using, for about 30 seconds. Scatter in the basil and coriander and cook until the herbs change colour slightly, 1–1½ minutes. Tip in the chopped tomatoes and lemon juice, bring to the boil and cook for a further 3–4 minutes. Remove from the heat and stir in the almonds, then set aside.

Preheat the oven to 230°C/gas mark 8. In a 3-litre baking dish or 40cm round dish, arrange the potato slices in a single layer, then spread the tomato–onion mixture thinly over the top. Follow with a single layer of the aubergine, then a second spread of the tomato–onion mixture, then the squash and then repeat this layering, ending with the aubergine. Arrange the fresh tomato slices on top. Add 500ml water to the remaining tomato–onion mixture and stir to incorporate. Drizzle this sauce all over the tomato slices and finish with the remaining olive oil. Cover with foil and bake until all of the liquid has evaporated, 40 minutes–1 hour. Serve with the Rice and Vermicelli Pilaf.

VARIATION *Split open a baguette or loaf of Italian bread and stuff with cold baked aubergine for a wonderful summer sandwich.*

SERVES 6–8

120ml extra virgin olive oil

2 medium white onions, chopped

4–5 garlic cloves, finely chopped

1 tablespoon ground allspice

1 tablespoon ground coriander

1 tablespoon freshly ground black pepper

1 teaspoon ground cumin (optional)

½ teaspoon hot or sweet paprika (optional)

30g chopped fresh basil

30g chopped fresh coriander

4 plum tomatoes, chopped, plus 5 plum tomatoes or 2 beefsteak tomatoes, thinly sliced

120ml fresh lemon juice

150g slivered almonds, toasted

3 baking potatoes (about 1.25kg in total), peeled and cut lengthways into 6mm-thick slices

3 Italian (baby) aubergines (1.25–1.5kg in total), sliced lengthways into 1.2cm-thick slices, fried or baked (page 39)

8 Arabic squash or courgettes, or 5 small seedless courgettes, cut lengthways into 1.2cm-thick slices

Rice and Vermicelli Pilaf (page 182) or Arabic Bread (page 57), for serving

EGGS IN PURGATORY

SHAKSHUKA

Most Middle Eastern countries, from Israel and Palestine to Algeria, Morocco and Tunisia, make a variation of this delicious peasant dish. It is an ideal option when you don't have anything in the cupboard – you break a few eggs into a simmering seasoned tomato sauce and it's time to eat. Stir in cooling plain yogurt and serve with Arabic bread for scooping up the sauce. It is delicious for breakfast, lunch or dinner, or as at Tanoreen, for Sunday brunch.

Place the oil in a large frying pan, over a medium-high heat and sauté the garlic and shallots until they begin to take on colour, about 3 minutes. Add the red and green peppers and cook for a further 3 minutes. Stir in the tomato purée and hot sauce until incorporated, about 3 minutes, then add the cumin, coriander, salt and caraway, if using, and stir for 1 minute. Add the tomatoes, reduce the heat and cook until the liquid is reduced and the sauce has thickened, 10–12 minutes.

Add the aubergine and lemon juice, raise the heat and bring to the boil. Break the eggs into the frying pan in a single layer, pushing the whites towards the yolk with a wooden spoon to keep them intact. Cook until the whites are opaque and the middle of the yolk is still slightly runny. Scoop the eggs and tomato sauce into bowls and serve with the Arabic bread and yogurt.

SERVES 6

6 tablespoons extra virgin olive oil

6 garlic cloves, finely chopped

2 shallots, finely chopped

1 red pepper, cored and diced

1 green pepper, cored and diced

3 tablespoons tomato purée

3 tablespoons Homemade Hot Sauce
  (page 194) or shop-bought seedless
  Middle Eastern or Turkish chilli paste

1 tablespoon ground cumin, or to taste

1 teaspoon ground coriander

1 teaspoon sea salt

¼ teaspoon ground caraway (optional)

6 ripe beefsteak tomatoes (about 2–2.5kg
  in total), peeled and chopped

1 medium aubergine, about 500g, peeled,
  cut into 2.5cm dice and roasted or fried
  (page 39; optional)

juice of ½ lemon

6 medium eggs

Arabic Bread (page 57) and natural yogurt,
  for serving

VEGETARIAN STUFFED VEGETABLES

· ▪ ·

KHUDRA MAHSHI

If a vegetable can be stuffed, an Arab cook will stuff it! It may seem odd when it comes to potatoes, but it is second nature to me since my mother never missed a chance to use them. This stuffing is rather traditional – feel free to play with the spices and herbs to suit your taste. But keep in mind that the softer the vegetable, the more loosely packed with stuffing it should be; if a vegetable like Arabic squash is overfilled, the vegetable will burst during cooking. To serve, either arrange the whole vegetables on dinner plates with the sauce on the side, or split them lengthways and drizzle the sauce over the top.

❧ **COOKING TIP** If you're not going to serve the vegetables right away, remove them from the sauce to prevent the rice mixture from overcooking. It continues to cook for about 15 minutes after it is removed from the heat.

Using an apple corer, remove the insides of the aubergines, squash, tomatoes and potatoes, reserving only the insides of the squash. Place the cored vegetables in a large bowl of cold salted water and set aside.

Place 120ml olive oil in a large frying pan over a medium-high heat and sauté the onions until soft and fragrant, about 3 minutes. Stir in the garlic, if using, until fragrant, 1 minute, then the allspice, black pepper, nutmeg and cumin, if using, about 30 seconds. Scatter in the parsley, coriander, dill and mint and cook until the coriander changes colour, about 1 minute. Stir in 2 tablespoons tomato purée, the reserved squash flesh, the chillies, if using, tomatoes and 2 tablespoons pomegranate molasses. Raise the heat and bring the mixture to the boil. Season to taste with salt. Remove from the heat and stir in the rice until thoroughly combined. Pour in half of the lemon juice and the remaining olive oil. Taste and adjust the seasonings.

Drain the vegetables soaking in cold water. Working with one vegetable at a time, pat it dry and spoon in the stuffing to within 1.2cm of the opening. Place the vegetables, vertically with the open end up, in a 5-litre pot. Repeat with remaining vegetables. Replace the reserved trimmed end to each vegetable. Add enough water to cover, the remaining 2 tablespoons each of tomato purée and pomegranate molasses, and the remaining lemon juice to the pot. Place a heatproof plate over the vegetables, then cover the pot and bring to the boil over a high heat. Reduce the heat and simmer until the rice is tender, 35–40 minutes.

Using a slotted spoon, remove the vegetables to a serving dish and spoon the sauce in the pot on the side.

SERVES 4

4 baby aubergines, rinsed, stem end trimmed and reserved

4 Arabic squash, rinsed, stem end trimmed and reserved

4 plum tomatoes, rinsed, stem end trimmed and reserved

4 baking potatoes, rinsed, narrow end trimmed and reserved

For the Stuffing

250ml extra virgin olive oil

2 medium white or red onions, diced

1 garlic clove, finely chopped (optional)

4½ teaspoons ground allspice

1 tablespoon freshly ground black pepper, or to taste

½ teaspoon ground nutmeg

1 teaspoon ground cumin (optional)

60g chopped fresh flat-leaf parsley

30g chopped fresh coriander

2 tablespoons chopped fresh dill

1 tablespoon dried mint

4 tablespoons tomato purée

1 jalapeño or long green chilli, cored, deseeded and diced (optional)

6 plum tomatoes, diced

4 tablespoons pomegranate molasses

sea salt, to taste

600g Egyptian rice or cracked wheat

juice of 2 lemons

AUBERGINE NAPOLEON

———— •◦• ————

One of the most popular items on the Tanoreen menu, this tower of crispy pesto-marinated aubergine slices spread with smoky baba ghanouj just might be the dish that inspired me to write this cookbook. It draws on the flavours of the Middle East and the Mediterranean, but the truth is, I created it to encourage my son to eat aubergine. He always loved fried courgette sticks, so I cut aubergine in the same shape and he was none the wiser (although here they're cut in rounds). This is a good example of how I have taken advantage of ingredients that are available to me in the States and married them with the classic preparations from my childhood.

Arrange the aubergine slices on two baking trays, sprinkle with salt and set aside for 30 minutes or until the auberbine begins to sweat. Pat the slices dry with kitchen paper and set aside.

In a large bowl, whisk together the pesto, olive oil, garlic and lemon juice. Add the aubergine, toss to coat and marinate at room temperature for at least 1 hour or overnight in the fridge.

Place the flour onto a shallow rimmed plate. In a medium bowl, whisk together the egg whites and 250ml water. Combine the panko, Parmigiano-Reggiano cheese, parsley and pepper on a second shallow plate.

Spread a sheet of greaseproof paper on a clean work surface. Working with one slice of aubergine at a time, dredge it in the flour first, shaking off the excess, and then dip it in the egg mixture followed by the breadcrumbs. Gently press the breadcrumbs onto both sides of the aubergine and place on the greaseproof paper. Repeat with the remaining aubergine slices.

Place at least 5cm vegetable oil in a small, deep pot over a high heat until hot but not smoking. Working in batches, fry the aubergine slices until golden, turning once, 3–5 minutes – do not crowd the pot. Using a slotted spoon, transfer the aubergine slices to a kitchen paper-lined platter to drain.

Place an aubergine slice on a small plate. Spread with 2 tablespoons baba ghanouj, top with a second aubergine slice and spread 1 tablespoon baba ghanouj on top. Repeat layering in this order with the remaining aubergine slices and baba ghanouj to make eight to ten aubergine stacks.

In a medium bowl, combine the tomatoes and onion. In a small bowl, whisk together the pesto, lemon juice, olive oil and salt. Drizzle just enough of the pesto mixture over the tomato-onion mixture to thoroughly coat. Spoon some salad around each Napoleon and drizzle each with some of the dressing left in the bottom of the bowl. Serve immediately.

SERVES 8–10

3 medium aubergines (1.25–1.5kg in total), stem and root ends trimmed and discarded, sliced into 1.2cm-thick rounds
sea salt, for sprinkling
60ml Basil Pesto (page 191)
120ml extra virgin olive oil
6 garlic cloves, finely chopped
juice of 3 lemons
60g plain flour
2 egg whites, beaten
200g panko (Japanese breadcrumbs)
2 tablespoons grated Parmigiano-Reggiano cheese
2 tablespoons dried parsley
½ teaspoon freshly ground black pepper
vegetable oil, for frying
750ml Baba Ghanouj (page 40) or Mutabal (page 41), for serving

For the Salad
8 plum tomatoes, chopped
1 medium red onion, chopped
7 tablespoons Basil Pesto (page 191)
juice of 2 lemons
180ml extra virgin olive oil
pinch of sea salt

VEGETARIAN STUFFED CABBAGE

—◆—

MALFOOF BELZAIT

I make these delicious rolls my mother's way, with cracked wheat rather than rice, which is what everyone back home uses. If you're gluten sensitive, rice is a nice alternative. I prefer using coarse bulgur, but slightly finer will work just as well. These rolls can be wrapped tightly and refrigerated for up to ten days, but they do not freeze well. Eat them at room temperature, or reheat them with a little water in a covered saucepan over a low heat. We never made just one meal's worth of these delicious stuffed leaves; they are delicious stuffed into Arabic Bread (page 57).

In a large bowl, combine the bulgur wheat with the parsley and all but 1 tablespoon of the garlic, the shallots, tomatoes, 1 tablespoon of the chillies, if using, half of the lemon juice, the oil, seedless Middle Eastern or Turkish chilli paste, if using, cumin, salt, pepper and allspice. Stir with a wooden spoon until thoroughly combined. Trim the tough ribs from the cabbage and stack the leaves on top of each other.

Line a 4-litre stockpot with a single layer of the potato slices (this prevents the cabbage leaves on the bottom layer from burning). Arrange the ribs of the cabbage on top of the potatoes. Working with one cabbage leaf at a time, place a leaf on a clean work surface with the stem end facing you. Spoon 2 tablespoons of the bulgur filling into the centre of the leaf, then roll the leaf away from you, tucking in the sides as you go. Arrange the rolls in the pot in concentric circles, beginning from the outer rim and working in. Stack them, one on top of another, to make a second layer.

Place a heatproof plate on top of the rolls, add enough water to the pot to cover both, about 750ml–1 litre of water, along with a pinch of salt. Cover the pot and bring to the boil over a high heat, then reduce the heat and simmer for 35–40 minutes.

Remove the pot from the heat, uncover and, wearing an oven glove, press the plate firmly against the cabbage and upend the pot to drain the cooking water into a large bowl. Stir the remaining 1 tablespoon garlic and the remaining lemon juice and chillies, if using, into the cooking water to create a stock. Remove the plate from the pot, pour the seasoned stock back into the pot and return it to the boil over a high heat for a further 1 minute. With a slotted spoon, transfer the rolls to a platter and serve.

VARIATION *Cabbage Lasagne If you don't have time to roll the stuffing into the cabbage leaves, prepare this dish as you would lasagne. Arrange a single layer of cabbage leaves on the bottom of an ungreased 3-litre baking dish and spread a third of the stuffing over the leaves. Toss a few garlic cloves over it. Cover the stuffing with a second layer of cabbage leaves. Continue layering the cabbage, stuffing and garlic cloves, ending with a layer of cabbage. Pour enough vegetable stock into the pan to just cover the top layer (about 1 litre) and bake at 175°C/gas mark 4 until the stock is absorbed, 35–40 minutes. Squeeze some fresh lemon juice over the cabbage lasagne and serve.*

SERVES 6–8 (WITH LEFTOVERS)

300g bulgur wheat, rinsed under warm water, or 400g Egyptian rice

25g chopped fresh flat-leaf parsley

6 garlic cloves, finely chopped

5 shallots, finely chopped

3 plum tomatoes, chopped

1 jalapeño or 2 long green chillies, finely chopped (optional)

juice of 3 lemons

120ml extra virgin olive oil

2 tablespoons seedless Middle Eastern or Turkish chilli paste (optional)

1 teaspoon ground cumin or to taste

1 tablespoon plus 1 pinch of sea salt

1 tablespoon freshly ground black pepper

1 tablespoon ground allspice

1 large green cabbage (about 2kg), boiled (page 156)

1 baking potato, or 2 tomatoes or carrots, sliced into 6mm-thick slices

TANOREEN BAKED FISH

—— ·•· ——

SAMAK BEL FURRON

I learned how to prepare this wonderful party dish from two men who worked for me at Tanoreen. Neither of them were cooks, but they often talked about the way their mothers baked fish. I borrowed their basic method and added some of my mother's touches – peppers, tomatoes and potatoes. I consider myself a very picky fish eater, but this is so good that I put it on the Tanoreen menu. If you are using fillets, buy the fish whole and ask the fishmonger to fillet it for you. Serve with Rice and Vermicelli Pilaf (page 182).

Preheat the oven to 200°C/gas mark 6.

In a small bowl, combine the garlic, half of the lemon juice, 120ml oil, the parsley or coriander, cumin, salt and pepper; set aside.

Using a sharp kitchen knife, make three 3mm slits across the length of each fish or on the skin-side of half of the fillets. Divide the spice mixture evenly among the fish and spread it with your fingers into the slits and cavity of the whole fish or in the slits and on the flesh side of the scored fillets.

Arrange the potatoes in a single layer in a large roasting tin and place the whole fish on top. If using the fillets, lay the plain halves skin-side down, then top each with a seasoned fillet, skin-side up. Scatter the tomatoes and peppers or chillies over the fish and pour the stock or water into one corner of the tin so that the vegetables don't slide off the fish. Drizzle the remaining oil and lemon juice over the fish, then cover tightly with greaseproof paper and foil and bake until the fish is opaque, 15–20 minutes, depending whether you're using a whole fish or fillets. Remove the foil and greaseproof paper and cook for a further 2 minutes, or until the fish flakes apart easily when pricked with a fork. Arrange the fish and potatoes on a serving dish and spoon the tin juices over both.

SERVES 6–8

9 garlic cloves, crushed

juice of 4–5 lemons

250ml extra virgin olive oil

60g chopped fresh flat-leaf parsley
   or coriander

4½ teaspoons ground cumin

1 tablespoon sea salt

1 tablespoon freshly ground black pepper

4–6 whole bass or flounders (500–600g
   each) or 8 fillets

8 medium red potatoes, peeled and
   sliced into 6mm rounds, fried or roasted

2 plum tomatoes, diced

2 green or red peppers or chillies,
   deseeded and chopped very fine

1 litre chicken stock or water

SPICY BAKED FISH

— ◆ —

SAMAKA HARRA

Samaka harra, literally translated, means 'hot fish'. The traditional preparation incorporates tahini in the sauce, but I am very fond of this version, which features crushed walnuts in the stuffing instead. This is a wonderful party dish – the whole baked fish makes for quite the conversation starter when set down in the middle of the table. Growing up, the fish was never boned – my father did it right at the table – but these days, it's more efficient to have the fishmonger debone it for you. Baking one whole fish is dramatic, but if you can't find a 2–2.5kg fish, use a duo of 1–1.5kg fish such as sea bass or bream. This makes a great meal served with my Tanoreen Green Salad (page 76) and rice.

Sprinkle salt all over the fish and rub it down under cold water; pat it dry and place on a clean work surface.

In a jar, combine the oil and lemon juice. In the bowl of a food processor, place half of the oil and lemon mixture with the ground coriander, black pepper, salt, cumin, if using, chilli, coriander, garlic and chilli paste and process until smooth. Add the walnuts and blitz until the mixture forms a chunky paste.

Preheat the oven to 230°C/gas mark 8. On one side of the fish, make two slits across, about 5cm apart and on the diagonal. Fill each slit with some of the walnut paste and spread all but 1 tablespoon of the remaining walnut paste into the cavity of the fish. Rub the reserved walnut paste all over the outside of the fish.

Transfer the fish to a roasting tin and drizzle with the remaining oil and lemon juice mixture. Cover the tin with greaseproof paper, then seal tightly with foil. Bake until the fish is no longer translucent and the skin is golden, 30–40 minutes for one large fish, depending on the desired doneness, or 20–25 minutes for two smaller fish. About 5 minutes before the fish is done, baste it with the pan juices.

Transfer the fish to a large serving dish and spoon the pan juices over it.

SERVES 4–6

1 tablespoon sea salt, plus extra for sprinkling

1 large or 2 small red snappers (2–2.5kg in total)

250ml extra virgin olive oil

160ml fresh lemon juice

1 tablespoon ground coriander

1 tablespoon freshly ground black pepper

½ tablespoon ground cumin (optional)

1 long green or jalapeño chilli, finely chopped

60g chopped fresh coriander or flat-leaf parsley

10 garlic cloves, crushed

2 tablespoons seedless Middle Eastern or Turkish chilli paste

225g crushed walnuts

FRESH FROM THE SEA

Sprinkling your fresh fish with salt and rubbing it down under running water takes care of any lingering fishy smell, resulting in cooking with fish as if it came fresh out of the sea.

FISHERMAN'S DISH

—— ••• ——

SAYADIYYA

Our weekend meals always had a kind of rhythm to them: Friday was the day the freshest fish was available at the market and every family bought far more than they needed for dinner that night. We were seven, which meant that my father bought not seven fish, but seventeen! *Sayadiyya* will always symbolise Saturday dinner to me; the dish was easy for my mother to pull together when she returned home from her day of teaching because we always had fried fish leftover from Friday's late supper. She would caramelise the onions on Friday night in the same oil that was used to fry the fish, and then pull the rest of the elements together on Saturday night. It is also my daughter's favourite way to eat fish.

⚜ **COOKING TIP** Take care not to turn the fish until it is well seared, and avoid crowding the pan or the fish will steam rather than fry properly.

In a small bowl, combine the salt, pepper, allspice and cumin. Rub a third of the spice mixture into the cavities of the whole fish or all over the fillets or prawns.

Place the vegetable oil in a heavy-bottomed pan over a high heat. When hot, fry two fish or a third of the prawns at a time, turning once without crowding them, until golden brown on both sides, 2–3 minutes per side. (Do not touch the fish until the underside is golden brown or the skin will stick to the bottom of the pan.) Using a slotted spatula, transfer the fish or prawns to a kitchen paper-lined platter.

Pour the vegetable oil through a sieve into a heatproof cup or bowl. Return this to the pan, add the olive oil, place over a medium-high heat and sauté the onions until they turn medium brown – take care not to burn them. Transfer 100g of the onions to a kitchen paper-lined plate and reserve. Add the garlic and sauté until soft and fragrant, about 30 seconds, then stir in the remaining spice mixture. Add the rice and stir until thoroughly coated, about 2 minutes. Remove the pan from the heat and tip in the tomatoes. Slowly pour in 1.5 litres boiling water. Reduce the heat, cover and simmer for 12 minutes, arranging the fish over the rice for the last 5 minutes of cooking. Alternatively, for a crispier fish, reheat it for 5 minutes in a 200°C/gas mark 6 oven.

To serve, spoon the rice onto the centre of a large platter and surround it with the fish. Scatter the reserved onions and the toasted almonds over the top.

SERVES 6

4½ teaspoons sea salt

1 tablespoon freshly ground black pepper

1 tablespoon ground allspice

1 tablespoon ground cumin

6 whole bass, or other white-fleshed fish (500g each), cleaned, or 1.5kg fillets, or 1kg shell-on prawns

250ml vegetable oil

250ml extra virgin olive oil

3 Spanish onions, thinly sliced (about 400g)

½ tablespoon finely chopped garlic

800g Egyptian or Chinese rice

100g cherry tomatoes

1.5 litres boiling water

150g slivered almonds, toasted

FISH TAGINE

—◦•◦—

SAMAK TAGINE

My mother never used coriander and hot sauce in the tagines she occasionally made on Saturday nights, but my version is certainly inspired by hers. Traditionally made with just tahini, caramelised onions, lemon juice and garlic, this popular fish dish is prepared when there's time available to spend in the kitchen. Serve with Rice and Vermicelli Pilaf (page 182), Arabic Bread (page 57) and a green salad.

Rub the fish all over with the salt under running water. Pat dry.

Place the vegetable oil in a heavy-bottomed pot over a medium-high heat. When hot, slip 2 whole fish or 4 fillets into the pot, taking care not to crowd them, and fry, turning once, until they are golden brown on both sides, 2–3 minutes per side. Do not touch the fish until the underside is golden brown or the skin will stick to the bottom of the pan. Using a slotted spatula, transfer the fish to a paper towel-lined platter.

Pour the vegetable oil through a strainer into a heatproof cup or bowl. Return this to the pot, add the olive oil, place over a medium-high heat and sauté the onions until they turn golden brown. Take care not to burn them. Set aside.

Preheat the oven to 230°C/gas mark 8. Meanwhile, in a large bowl, combine the tahini sauce, stock, coriander, garlic, shallots, if using, chilli paste, pepper and cumin and whisk together.

Arrange the fried fish in a large roasting pan and scatter the onions on top. Tuck the potatoes and peppers around the fish, then pour over the tahini mixture. Cover the pan tightly with foil and roast until the fish flakes easily when pricked with a fork, about 20 minutes. Remove the foil and roast for a further 5 minutes. Transfer to a platter and serve immediately, garnished with the parsley or coriander.

SERVES 6

6 whole red snappers or bass (about 500g each), gutted, scaled and trimmed, or 12 fillets
sea salt, for sprinkling
250ml vegetable oil
180ml extra virgin olive oil
2 Spanish onions, thinly sliced
625ml Thick Tahini Sauce (page 195)
500ml stock from Seasoned Chicken with Stock (page 90)
60g chopped coriander
6 garlic cloves, finely chopped
2 shallots, diced (optional)
1 tablespoon seedless Middle Eastern or Turkish chilli paste
1 tablespoon freshly ground black pepper
1 tablespoon ground cumin
6 white potatoes, peeled and cut into 1.2cm cubes
½ green or red pepper, deseeded and diced
chopped fresh flat-leaf parsley and coriander, for garnish

FRIDAY FISH-FRIES

Whole fried fish holds a special place in my heart, as it has been a culinary constant throughout my life. My love affair with it began in Nazareth, followed me to New York and then zigzagged with me throughout Europe. I've had some of the best times in my life sitting around a table set with platters of crispy, succulent fish. In fact, it was during one of these meals, almost fourteen years ago, that my girlfriends convinced me to open a restaurant. We gathered at least once a month in my Brooklyn kitchen for an *arak*-soaked fish fry. There were platters piled high with crispy fried red snapper, hand-cut chips, chopped tomato salad flecked with jalapeño, bowls of quartered lemons, boats of parsley-tahini sauce and lots of prodding from them, encouraging me to turn what I loved doing into a business. And here we are.

To this day, gathering around a table of fried fish conjures crystal clear memories of the Friday fish dinners we ate at home in Nazareth. These suppers were as much a series of rituals as they were a meal. To get the freshest catch, my father woke up before the sun rose to be one of the first customers at the fishmonger's counter. He usually bought *mushout*, a fish similar to bream, from Lake Tiberias in northern Galilee, but there was also bass, and delicate barbonies.

In the evening, my mother hauled out the big pot she reserved for frying fish, filled it part way with olive oil and set it on the stove. While the oil was heating up, she salted the fish. I used to love the crackling sound the hot oil made when the fish hit it, but nothing was more exciting than watching her remove the golden, crispy fish with her big spoon to a platter. It was only a matter of seconds before my family and, more often than not, a few neighbours and friends, were picking the fish apart, scooping it up with pitta and dipping it into parsley-tahini sauce. We were a noisy bunch, talking, laughing and telling stories as the adults sipped arak. I remember my father deboning the fish for the little ones, as I did when I made this whole fish for my young children at home in Brooklyn.

These days most fried fish is eaten in restaurants. Nazareth is full of places that specialise in the dish. If home cooks do want to prepare whole fried fish, they do it in an outdoor fryer, which is a good option and makes for great entertaining.

'TO THIS DAY, GATHERING AROUND A TABLE OF FRIED FISH CONJURES CRYSTAL CLEAR MEMORIES OF THE FRIDAY FISH DINNERS WE ATE AT HOME IN NAZARETH. THESE SUPPERS WERE AS MUCH A SERIES OF RITUALS AS THEY WERE A MEAL.'

WHOLE FRIED FISH

— ❖ —

SAMAK MAQLEH

I remember my mother frying fish in olive oil, then using it to fry pieces of bread. She served the golden brown nuggets with a tahini-parsley sauce, for dipping. These days, I fry fish in vegetable oil. While it is delicious prepared simply – seasoned with salt and pepper followed by a quick dredge in flour – I prefer to spice things up a bit by making slits in the flesh and stuffing them with *tetbileh*, a sauce of garlic, chilli, lemon juice and olive oil. My favourite fish to fry include red snapper, bass, bream and red mullet. Serve this with Thick Tahini Sauce, (page 195), Tomato Salad (page 69) or Fried Tomatoes (page 176). Use any leftover fish to make Fish Tagine (page 126) or Fisherman's Dish (page 125).

Rub the fish all over with salt under cold running water. Pat dry. Make the *tetbileh*: Mix all the ingredients in a food processor and pulse into a coarse mixture. To store, transfer to a container with a tight-fitting lid, top with olive oil and refrigerate for up to 2 weeks.

Using a sharp kitchen knife, make three 3mm-deep slits across the length of each fish. Using your fingers, rub 1 tablespoon of the *tetbileh* into the slits and cavity of each fish. Set aside.

Place the flour in a large shallow plate. Working with one fish at a time, dredge it in the flour, using it to seal the cavity shut. Shake off the excess and set aside on greaseproof paper.

Place the vegetable oil in a large, heavy-bottomed pot over a high heat. When hot, fry one or two fish at a time, turning once without crowding them, until they are golden brown on both sides, 2–3 minutes per side. Do not touch the fish until the underside is golden brown or the skin will stick to the bottom of the pan. Using a slotted spatula, transfer the fish to a kitchen paper-lined platter. Serve warm with the lemon halves.

SERVES 4

4 whole fish of choice (500–750g each), cleaned
sea salt, for sprinkling
60ml *Tetbileh* (see below)
125g plain white flour
1 litre vegetable oil
3 lemons, halved

For the *Tetbileh*
(Makes about 320ml)
10 garlic cloves, chopped into a coarse paste
2 long hot or jalapeño peppers, finely chopped
1 tablespoon paprika
1 tablespoon black pepper
1 tablespoon cumin
120ml extra virgin olive oil
4 tablespoons fresh lemon juice
1 tablespoon salt
handful of chopped fresh flat-leaf parsley

PRAWNS IN GARLIC SAUCE

My arrival in New York was full of firsts, including tasting prawns for the first time. Wafa was certain that I would love them, especially the way they were prepared at a seafood restaurant he had eaten at in Sheepshead Bay, Brooklyn. He was wrong. But I came to love the shellfish over the years after preparing them my way – in a flavourful garlic sauce – at home.

This is a great dish to make on a busy weeknight, as it takes all of ten minutes to prepare if you ask your fishmonger to peel and devein the prawns for you. It requires even less time if he or she butterflies them. Serve the prawns over Rice and Vermicelli Pilaf (page 182) and with Arabic Bread (page 57) or a baguette for dipping into the sauce.

Place the olive oil in a large frying pan over a medium heat. When hot but not smoking, sauté the prawns until the bottoms lose their pink colour, about 90 seconds. Add the garlic, turn the prawns and sauté for a further 90 seconds. Stir in all but 2 tablespoons of the parsley, the paprika, salt and pepper and sauté until fragrant, about 1 minute. Pour in the stock or water and lemon juice and bring to the boil. Add the ghee or butter, if using, and the breadcrumbs and return to the boil for 2 minutes.

Arrange the prawns over the rice and vermicelli pilaf and spoon some of the stock over both. Serve with Arabic bread, a scattering of parsley and lemon wedges.

SERVES 6

80ml extra virgin olive oil
1kg prawns, peeled, deveined and butterflied
10 garlic cloves, finely chopped
60g chopped fresh flat-leaf parsley
1 teaspoon paprika, optional
1 teaspoon sea salt
1 teaspoon freshly ground black pepper
500ml stock from Seasoned Chicken with Stock (page 90), or water
juice of 2 lemons, or to taste
3 tablespoons ghee or butter (optional)
3 tablespoons dried breadcrumbs
Rice and Vermicelli Pilaf (page 182), for serving
Arabic bread (page 57), for serving
lemon wedges, for garnish

SALMON IN PESTO

—— •◆• ——

Before I came to the US, the only way I had ever eaten salmon was smoked. My father would bring some home on very rare occasions; it simply wasn't readily available. Several months into Tanoreen's first year, I noticed that some customers would nervously scan the menu in search of a familiar dish. I created this with them in mind. Serve with Rice and Vermicelli Pilaf (page 182).

In a small bowl, combine 1½ teaspoons coriander, ½ teaspoon pepper and ½ teaspoon salt. Season the salmon on both sides with this spice mixture and arrange the fish in a roasting tin, skin-side down if using fillets, spacing them 5 cm apart. Set aside.

Preheat the oven to 230°C/gas mark 8.

Place 120ml oil in a large frying pan over a medium-high heat and sauté the garlic until golden and fragrant, about 2 minutes. Add the artichoke hearts and cook, turning until browned all over, about 6 minutes in total. Tip in the tomatoes and remaining pepper, coriander and salt and cook until the tomatoes soften slightly and release their juices, about 5 minutes. Stir in the pesto and lemon juice and return to the boil for 2 minutes.

Using a slotted spoon, transfer the artichoke mixture to the roasting tin, tucking them in between the salmon fillets. Pour the sauce over the salmon and drizzle the remaining oil on top. Gently add the chicken stock to the tin by pouring it in at one corner so as not to wash the oil away. Cover the pan with foil and bake for 15 minutes. Remove the foil and bake for a further 2 minutes or until the salmon is cooked to the desired doneness.

To serve, transfer the fillets to dinner plates and spoon some of the sauce from the tin over them. Garnish with the parsley and lemon wedges.

SERVES 6

1 tablespoon ground coriander

1 teaspoon freshly ground black pepper

1 teaspoon sea salt, plus extra to taste

6 salmon fillets, skin on, or 5cm-thick steaks

250ml olive oil

8 garlic cloves, finely chopped

2 bags (500g each) frozen artichoke hearts, thawed and cut into 1.2cm-thick pieces

8 plum tomatoes, diced

180ml Basil Pesto (page 191)

juice of 2–3 lemons (about 120ml)

375ml stock from Seasoned Chicken with Stock (page 90)

15g chopped fresh flat-leaf parsley and 1 lemon, cut into wedges, for garnish

GRILLED RED SNAPPER IN GRAPE LEAVES

—— ·✦· ——

I decided to wrap fish in vine leaves after a visit to Jerusalem for Jumana's christening. For the celebration dinner, there was kafta wrapped in the briny greens, which imparted a delightful tang to the meat. Not only do the leaves do the same for fish, they also keep it moist. The marinade is excellent for all manner of fish and chicken.

Using a sharp kitchen knife, make three 3mm slits across the length of both sides of each fish. Set aside.

In a large baking dish, combine the oil and lemon juice with the garlic, shallots, tomatoes, sesame oil, jalapeño, if using, oregano, cumin, coriander and black pepper. Arrange the fish in the dish and, using your hands, rub the marinade into the slits and into the cavity of each fish. Cover the dish tightly and refrigerate overnight, turning the fish once or twice.

Prepare a gas or charcoal grill (or preheat the grill on your oven). On a clean work surface, spread out a piece of foil several centimetres longer and wider than one fish and place an equal-sized piece of greaseproof paper on top. Arrange 6–8 vine leaves on the greaseproof paper, overlapping them to form a rectangular shape. Place a fish in the centre of the vine leaves and fold the vine leaves onto it like an envelope. Reserving the marinade, fold up the fish in the greaseproof paper and then the foil, wrapping it tightly. Place the packets on the grill and cook for 7–10 minutes per side.

Place the marinade in a medium pan over a high heat and reduce to a sauce. Using kitchen scissors, cut through the foil and greaseproof paper to open the packets, then transfer each wrapped fish to a dinner plate and serve with the marinade and a squeeze of lemon.

SERVES 4–6

4–6 whole red snapper (500g each), boned or bone-in
80ml extra virgin olive oil
juice of 5 lemons
6 garlic cloves, finely chopped
3 shallots, finely chopped
2 plum tomatoes, finely chopped
2 tablespoons dark sesame oil
1 jalapeño chilli, deseeded, if desired, and finely chopped
1 tablespoon chopped fresh oregano
1 tablespoon ground cumin
1 tablespoon ground coriander
1 tablespoon freshly ground black pepper
6–8 vine leaves per fish, rinsed
lemon wedges, for garnish

ROASTED FISH

— ✦ —

SAMAK MHAMMAR

I was inspired by the ingredients used in the quintessential Palestinian dish, *Musakhan* (page 142) when I created this version of roasted fish. Slathered in tangy sumac and my fiery Homemade Hot Sauce (page 194), the mellow fish comes alive with Middle Eastern flavours. Serve with the Tanoreen Green Salad (page 76).

Preheat the oven to 230°C/gas mark 8.

Place the oil in a large frying pan over a medium-high heat. When hot, sauté the onions until golden, 7–10 minutes. Transfer the onions to a small bowl and add the lemon juice, sumac, hot sauce, allspice, pepper and cumin and mix well.

Slice the fish open like a book and spread 5 tablespoons of the onion mixture into each. Transfer to a roasting tin. Cover the tin tightly with greaseproof paper and foil and roast until the fish is just cooked through, 10–15 minutes. Transfer to a serving dish and sprinkle with the almonds and pine nuts.

SERVES 6

80ml extra virgin olive oil

3 red or white onions, finely chopped

juice of 3 lemons

1 tablespoon sumac

1 tablespoon Homemade Hot Sauce (page 194) or seedless Middle Eastern or Turkish chilli paste

1 tablespoon ground allspice

1 tablespoon freshly ground black pepper

1 teaspoon ground cumin

4–6 whole sea bream (about 450g each)

75g slivered almonds

75g pine nuts, toasted

WHOLE STUFFED CHICKEN

DJAJ MAHSHI

This is a lavish special-occasion dish that is traditionally prepared for Easter but makes an excellent dinner-party dish as well. The beauty of stuffed chicken is that it can be the basis for several courses. After it is stuffed and seared on the hob, you can add chopped fresh parsley and additional stock or water to the drippings to make a quick soup to serve while the chicken is roasting. You will have more stuffing than you need for the two chickens. Transfer the remaining stuffing to a dish and serve with the chicken, along with some yogurt.

With the rack arranged in the centre, preheat the oven to 230°C/gas mark 8.

In a small bowl, combine the allspice, salt, pepper, nutmeg and cardamom. Using your hands, rub the spice mixture all over the inside and outside of the chickens. Spoon the stuffing into the cavity of each chicken, packing in as much filling as each will hold. Seal the cavities shut with cocktail sticks or short wooden skewers. Set aside the remaining stuffing.

Fill a deep roasting tin half full with water and set a rack in it. Rub each chicken all over with the oil and place them, side by side, on the rack. Bake the chickens until the water comes to the boil, then continue boiling for 15 minutes. Reduce the heat to 175°C/gas mark 4. Cover the roasting tin with foil and bake until the thigh juices run clear, about 1 hour 15 minutes.

Remove the foil, turn on the grill and slide the roasting tin under the grill. Grill the chickens until the skin is golden brown, turning once, about 5 minutes. Transfer to a carving board to rest.

For a first course, spoon the cooking liquid into soup bowls, add a little of the stuffing that has tumbled out of the chicken, stir in some parsley and serve with lemon wedges. Offer the stuffed chicken as a second course, served with natural yogurt on the side.

SERVES 6-8

1 tablespoon ground allspice

1 tablespoon sea salt

1 tablespoon freshly ground black pepper

1 level teaspoon freshly grated nutmeg

½ teaspoon ground cardamom

2 chickens (1.5kg each), rinsed and patted dry

Meat Stuffing (page 150), cooled

1-2 tablespoons extra virgin olive oil

6 bay leaves

chopped fresh flat-leaf parsley, for garnish

lemon wedges and natural yogurt, for serving

CHICKEN FETTI

—— •◆• ——

FETIT DJAJ

The word *fetti* is derived from the Arabic word *fetafiit*, meaning 'crumbled'; in this case, crumbled squares of toasted pitta covered with a tangy yogurt-tahini sauce. There are endless variations on fetti, including those prepared with aubergine, chickpeas or lamb. Back home in Nazareth, we ate *kroush fetti*, made with boiled lamb stomach. Egyptians make *fetti* without any yogurt at all; they use a mix of vinegar, garlic and chillies. My Syrian friends in New York introduced me to this chicken version, which can be prepared in advance and assembled just before serving.

In a small bowl, combine the allspice, pepper, salt, and nutmeg in a small bowl. Rub half of the spice mixture all over the chicken pieces.

Place 120ml oil in a 5-litre casserole over a medium-high heat and sauté the chicken pieces until brown all over, leaving them untouched for at least 2–3 minutes to prevent sticking. Add the cinnamon stick, cardamom, cloves, bay leaves and onion, then 3 litres water, along with the reserved neck and giblets. Increase the heat, bring to the boil, then reduce the heat and simmer for 1 hour. Using a slotted spoon, skim the foam that rises to the surface every 15 minutes.

Transfer the chicken to a platter and set aside to cool. Strain the stock, discard the solids and return the stock to a gentle simmer in the pot. When the chicken is cool enough to handle, discard the skin and remove the meat from the bones. Shred the chicken and sprinkle it with 250ml stock to prevent it from drying out; cover loosely and set aside.

In a second large, heavy-bottomed pot, combine the remaining oil and ghee or butter and place over a medium-high heat. Add the vermicelli to the pot – if using a nest of vermicelli, break it up with your hands first – then sauté the noodles, stirring constantly, until golden brown. Add the rice and stir constantly until the grains turn pearly white. Pour in 2 litres of the simmering stock and stir in the remaining spice mixture. Cover and simmer for 12 minutes, stirring twice. Remove from the heat, cover and set aside, undisturbed, for 5 minutes.

Meanwhile, make the yogurt sauce: In the bowl of a food processor, combine the tahini sauce, yogurt, garlic and lemon juice, if needed; pulse until a smooth sauce forms. Alternatively, combine in a large bowl and mix with a hand mixer until smooth. Transfer to a saucepan and bring to a simmer over a medium heat. Do not boil.

To serve, spoon the rice into the centre of a large serving dish, shaping it into a mound and leaving a 1–2cm rim around the edge. Top with the chicken, then spoon the warm sauce over it all. Arrange the bread around the rim and garnish with the nuts and parsley.

SERVES 6–8

2 tablespoons ground allspice

1 tablespoon freshly ground black pepper

5½ teaspoons sea salt

½ teaspoon grated fresh nutmeg

250ml olive oil

2 chickens (1.5–2kg), cut into 4 pieces (reserve neck, skin and all giblets but the liver for stock)

1 cinnamon stick

5 whole cardamom pods

5 whole cloves

3 bay leaves

1 white onion, peeled

4 tablespoons ghee or 8 tablespoons butter

500g round vermicelli

900g short-grain rice such as Egyptian or Basmati

For the Yogurt Sauce
Thick Tahini Sauce (page 195)

500ml natural low-fat yogurt

2 garlic cloves, crushed

juice of 1 lemon, if needed

For Serving
6 (20cm) pieces Arabic bread, toasted (page 57)

150g slivered almonds, toasted

75–150g pine nuts, toasted

30g chopped fresh flat-leaf parsley

EGYPTIAN FETTI SAUCE

🍴 **COOKING TIPS** Leftovers can be reheated with a little water to thin the yogurt sauce. Simmer gently, being careful not to let the sauce boil, which will cause it to separate.

If you are using shop-bought yogurt, be sure to include the lemon. If you are making your own, omit it. I find if I make yogurt with room-temperature milk, it tastes pleasingly sour. Cold milk produces yogurt that's on the sweeter side.

For customers who don't eat dairy, I make the *fetti* sauce the Egyptian way. It is a wonderful substitute for the tahini-based sauce and can be used not only on chicken, but with beef or lamb, too.

2 tablespoons extra virgin olive oil, ghee or butter
6 garlic cloves, finely chopped
2 chillies, finely chopped
1 tablespoon ground coriander
1 teaspoon sea salt
½ teaspoon freshly ground black pepper
80ml distilled white vinegar
juice of 1 lemon

Place the oil, ghee or butter in a small frying pan over a medium-high heat and stir in the garlic, chillies, coriander, salt and black pepper until fragrant, about 30 seconds. Turn off the heat and stir in the vinegar, then return the heat to high. Bring to the boil, add the lemon juice, reduce to a simmer and remove the pan from the heat.

139

THE ROMANCE OF MAFTOOL

My father was a rather chivalrous man, particularly when it came to my mother. His gestures were not necessarily showy or grand, but they were nothing if not charming.

One of my favourite memories of my parents is tied to the ritual of making *maftool*, a pasta that is often incorrectly referred to as 'Israeli couscous' here in America. Given how much patience and diligence is required to make the grains by hand, it is clear proof to me just how important food was and remains to our culture.

In our Nazareth home, making this pearly pasta started early in the morning. The first step was roasting and grinding her own spices. The aroma of caraway, anise and cumin floated in the air. My mother filled a huge stockpot with either lamb bones or whole chickens, vegetables, the spices and water. While the water came to the boil, she shaped the pasta. She stood while rolling a bit of wheat flour with drips of water in the palms of her hands, over a sieve continuously sprinkling flour and water in her palm until the granules were the size of rifle pellets. She would then coat the pasta with clarified butter to prevent the grains from sticking together while they steamed in a colander set in the pot of boiling stock. The fragrant stock perfumed the *maftool* before the two were combined in a bowl. Layering flavours this way was the key to my mother's memorable cooking. She insisted on spicing and perfuming every component of a dish.

Maftool is made with what seems like an absurd amount of silverskin onions. Peeling them is one of the most time-consuming steps in making the dish. For my parents, though, it was the most charmed. Because he hated to see her cry, my father always stepped in to tackle the mountain of onions on the kitchen counter. This may not seem especially gallant these days, but back then, men simply did not carry their weight in the kitchen. Watching my dad peel all those onions made me swoon. As a little girl, it just seemed so romantic!

The most endearing part of the process was not that my father saved my mom the burning eyes and endless tears, but that he'd close the kitchen door while he was preparing all of those onions because he didn't like anyone seeing *him* cry.

'WATCHING MY DAD PEEL ALL THOSE ONIONS MADE ME SWOON. AS A LITTLE GIRL, IT JUST SEEMED SO ROMANTIC!'

PALESTINIAN COUSCOUS WITH CHICKEN, CHICKPEAS AND PEARL ONIONS

MAFTOOL

It used to be that the whole family gathered to make homemade *maftool*. These days, almost no one makes it by hand, which is not surprising, since the process is very involved. *Maftool* is truly a one-dish meal – there are never pickles, sauces or salads served with it because the chicken, chickpeas and onions are like side dishes themselves. I prefer fresh silverskin onions, but if you need to speed things up, use the frozen variety.

In a small bowl, combine the caraway, allspice, cumin, coriander, salt, pepper, nutmeg, cardamom and cinnamon. Rub half of the spice mixture all over the chicken. Set aside the other half.

Place 6 tablespoons oil in a large, heavy-bottomed pan over a medium heat. Slip the chicken pieces into the pan, skin-side down, and sear, leaving them untouched for 6–8 minutes, until golden brown. Turn over and sear the other sides, a further 5 minutes. Using a slotted spoon, transfer the chicken to a plate and set aside. Sauté the silverskin and white onions until they begin to take on colour, 5–7 minutes, then return the chicken to the pot. Add the chickpeas and 3 litres water, raise the heat and bring to the boil. Reduce the heat and, using a spoon, skim off the foam from the top, trying not to skim off any spices along with it. Cover and simmer until the chicken is about to fall off the bone, 45 minutes–1 hour. Add the lemon juice, remove the pan from the heat and set aside.

Meanwhile, place the remaining olive oil in a large frying pan over a medium-high heat and sauté the rice until the grains are snowy white. Add the reserved spice mixture and stir until fragrant. Add 1.5 litres of the chicken stock from the pan and bring to the boil. Reduce the heat, cover and simmer until the rice is soft, adding more stock as needed, 15–20 minutes.

To serve, spoon the rice onto a large serving dish and arrange the chicken, chickpeas and onions around it.

SERVES 4

6 teaspoons ground caraway seeds
1 tablespoon ground allspice
1 tablespoon ground cumin
1 tablespoon ground coriander
1 tablespoon sea salt, or to taste
1 tablespoon freshly ground black pepper
½ teaspoon ground nutmeg
½ teaspoon ground cardamom
½ teaspoon ground cinnamon
1 chicken (1.25–1. kg), cut into
    4 or 8 pieces
10 tablespoons olive oil
1kg fresh silverskin onions, peeled
4 white onions, chopped
500g dried chickpeas, soaked (page 21)
    overnight and boiled or 2 (400g) tins,
    drained and rinsed
juice of ½ lemon
1kg *maftool* (see opposite) or Egyptian rice

CHICKEN 'PIZZA'

— ·•· —

MUSAKHAN

One of the most popular Tanoreen menu items, this traditional dish was originally made by serving a whole roasted chicken, smothered with onions, on a 40cm loaf of flatbread. Each diner would be served a big piece of the chicken, a torn piece of bread and a small mound of onions. Typically, they'd eat the dish with their hands, using the bread as a scoop. To make it easier to serve and eat (and because such a large flatbread, known as *taboun*, is difficult to find), I developed this 'user-friendly', pizza-style version of *musakhan*. It makes an excellent starter, cut into small wedges. Naan or Turkish flatbread also work nicely here.

In a small bowl, combine the sumac, allspice, salt, cardamom, cumin and nutmeg and set aside.

Place 80ml oil in a large frying pan over a medium heat and sauté half of the spice mixture until fragrant, about 30 seconds. Add the chicken to the frying pan and cook, stirring occasionally, until the chicken loses its pink colour, about 7 minutes.

In another frying pan, place 80ml oil over a medium heat and cook the remaining spice mixture, stirring, until fragrant, about 10 seconds. Add the onions and sauté until soft and golden, 2–3 minutes. Transfer the onion mixture, scraping the pan to catch all of the spices, to the chicken pot and stir with a wooden spoon to thoroughly combine. Pour in the remaining oil and simmer for 3–4 minutes.

Meanwhile, preheat the oven to 230°C/gas mark 8. Arrange the flatbreads on two baking sheets. Divide the chicken and onion mixture evenly among them, spreading within 6mm of the rim, then bake until warmed through, about 5 minutes. Remove from the oven and sprinkle the top of each pizza with 1½ teaspoons each of the nuts. Add a drizzle of lemon juice, if desired, and serve.

SERVES 6

2 heaped tablespoons sumac,
   or to taste
1 tablespoon ground allspice
1 tablespoon sea salt
¾ teaspoon ground cardamom
¼ teaspoon ground cumin
¼ teaspoon grated fresh nutmeg
250ml extra virgin olive oil
2 whole boneless, skinless chicken breasts
   (1.5kg in total), cut into 2.5cm pieces
4 white onions, chopped
6 Arabic Breads (page 57) or Greek,
   Turkish or Indian flatbreads
3 tablespoons slivered almonds, toasted
3 tablespoons pine nuts, toasted
juice of 2 lemons (optional)

CHICKEN WITH POTATOES

◦•◦

MHAMMAR

Every culture has a hearty chicken and potato dish. This one is in every Palestinian cook's repertoire, perhaps because it is so easy to make. I can't say that this version is entirely traditional, as I tend to use spices more liberally than most because I think they give the dish a little more dimension. *Mhammar* is very forgiving, which is why no two cooks use exactly the same ingredients. If you like heat, add 2 tablespoons of red chilli paste when sautéing the onions. It is also an excellent make-ahead dish; cover and refrigerate it, then when you're ready, warm in a 160°C/gas mark 3 oven until heated through. Serve with Arabic Bread (page 57), Rice and Vermicelli Pilaf (page 182) and a Tanoreen Green Salad (page 76).

In a large pot, bring the stock to a simmer.

Preheat the oven to 230°C/gas mark 8. Arrange the potatoes in a single layer in a large roasting tin, then set aside.

In the large frying pan used to fry the potatoes, reheat the reserved frying oil (if potatoes were roasted, heat the olive oil) over a medium-high heat. When hot, sauté the onions until golden and caramelised, 3–5 minutes. Add the chillies, if using, and cook until fragrant, 1 minute, then the sumac, allspice, lemon juice and 1 litre of the simmering chicken stock. Bring to the boil, then reduce to a simmer for 5 minutes. Remove from the heat.

Arrange the chicken pieces over the potatoes in the roasting tin. Pour the onion mixture over the top, then add the remaining simmering stock, pouring it slowly into the corner so as not to wash away the oil. Cover the pan with foil and bake for 20 minutes. Reduce the heat to 150°C/gas mark 2 and bake for a further 20 minutes. Serve warm with the lemon wedges.

SERVES 6–8

1.5 litres stock and the meat, skinned and chopped, from Seasoned Chicken with Stock (page 90)

8 baking potatoes peeled, cut into 6mm-thick slices and fried or roasted, frying oil reserved

120ml extra virgin olive oil (if using roasted potatoes)

6 white onions, diced

2 chillies, deseeded and finely diced (optional)

2 tablespoons sumac

1 tablespoon ground allspice

juice of 2 lemons

lemon wedges, for garnish

CHICKEN TAGINE

TAGINE DJAJ

This is the Tanoreen version of the iconic Moroccan dish. I didn't grow up eating tagine, but after dining in restaurants in Morocco, and in Tunisian restaurants in Paris, Marbella and New York, I grew to love the mix of dried fruits, vegetables and chicken. Of course, Moroccans don't use basil or apricots in their tagines; their recipe features currants, cherries, raisins or plums. I happen to love the combination of dried apricots and cranberries, which make a very flavourful sauce when slow-cooked with lots of spices. The ingredients list for this is long and the cooking is slow, but for the amount of active cooking time involved, the results are worth every minute. This tastes even better reheated as leftovers.

Preheat the oven to 250°C/gas mark 9.

In a small bowl, combine the allspice, coriander, turmeric, salt, pepper, cumin, saffron, nutmeg and cardamom. Rinse the chicken pieces and pat dry, then rub half the spice mixture all over. Set aside the other half.

Place 120ml oil in a large frying pan over a medium-high heat. When hot and working in batches, sear the chicken on all sides, about 4 minutes in total. Using a slotted spoon, remove the chicken from the pan to a plate.

In the same frying pan, sauté the onions until soft and fragrant, about 5 minutes. Stir in the garlic until fragrant, about 3 minutes., then the reserved spice mixture, about 1 minute. Scatter over the coriander, basil and parsley and stir until distributed throughout. Add the remaining oil with the dried fruits, lemon juice, chilli paste, olives and 1 litre water and bring to a simmer. Cook, stirring, for 2 minutes.

Meanwhile, arrange the carrots, silverskin onions and potatoes on the bottom of a large roasting tin. and place the chicken on top. Add the onion mixture and toss to thoroughly coat the chicken and vegetables. Set aside to marinate for 45–60 minutes. Cover the roasting tin with foil and bake until the chicken begins to sizzle, 10–15 minutes. Reduce the temperature to 175°C/gas mark 4 and bake for a further 30 minutes, then remove the foil and roast for a further 5 minutes.

Spoon the rice into the middle of a large platter and arrange the chicken, vegetables, fruits and all the tin juices around it. Garnish with the nuts and serve.

SERVES 6–8

1 tablespoon ground allspice

1 tablespoon ground coriander

1 tablespoon turmeric

1 tablespoon sea salt

1½ teaspoons freshly ground black pepper

1 teaspoon ground cumin

1 teaspoon saffron

¾ teaspoon ground nutmeg

½ teaspoon ground cardamom

2 chickens (1.25–1.5kg each), each cut into halves or quarters

250ml extra virgin olive oil

3 Spanish onions, chopped

8 garlic cloves, finely chopped

60g chopped fresh coriander

60g chopped fresh basil

60g chopped fresh flat-leaf parsley

120g chopped dried fruits, preferably apricots and cranberries

120ml fresh lemon juice

2 tablespoons seedless Middle Eastern or Turkish chilli paste

100g pitted and chopped Kalamata or green olives

500g baby carrots or whole carrots, chopped

500g silverskin onions, peeled

4 white potatoes, halved lengthways and sliced into half moons

Basmati Vegetable Rice (page 183), for serving

slivered almonds and pine nuts, for garnish

CHICKEN KEBABS

— ◆ —

SHISH TAWOOK

To serve these kebabs the traditional way, remove the skewer, wrap a pitta around the chicken, top with pickles and chopped lettuce and drizzle with the garlic sauce. At Tanoreen, I serve them over Rice and Vermicelli Pilaf (page 182) along with a Tanoreen Green Salad (page 76). Sometimes I punctuate every two pieces of chicken by adding a silverskin onion, cherry tomato or piece of pepper to the skewer. If using wooden skewers, soak them in water first for at least 30 minutes so they won't burn on the grill.

In a large bowl, combine the lemon juice and oil with the garlic, allspice, salt, pepper, cumin, nutmeg and paprika and mix well. Add the chicken and stir to coat with the marinade. Cover and refrigerate for at least 3 hours or overnight.

Prepare a gas or charcoal grill (or preheat the grill on your oven); it should be moderately hot. Divide the chicken evenly among 12 skewers, threading the pieces onto them so that they are fairly tightly packed. Grill over a moderate heat, turning three to four times until the chicken is cooked through and browned all over, 10–15 minutes depending on the heat of the grill and the distance from the heat source. Serve with the garlic sauce along with the pickles, lettuce and Arabic bread.

VARIATION *To make the kebabs the Indian way, add 250ml low-fat natural yogurt to the marinade ingredients. The yogurt is a wonderful tenderiser and imparts a gorgeous colour to the chicken pieces when grilled.*

SERVES 6

250ml fresh lemon juice
120ml extra virgin olive oil
10 garlic cloves, crushed
1 tablespoon ground allspice
1 tablespoon sea salt
1 teaspoon freshly ground black pepper
½ teaspoon ground cumin
¼ teaspoon ground nutmeg
½ teaspoon ground paprika
2kg boneless, skinless chicken breasts,
    cut into 2.5 x 4cm chunks
Garlic Sauce (page 191)
pickles, for garnish
lettuce, chopped, for garnish
Arabic bread (page 57), for serving

GRILLED QUAIL

Quail is a special-occasion food – in the same way that foie gras is. There is not a lot of meat on quail, so I tend to serve two to three per person, depending on the size of the quail. You can adjust the amount as you prefer. To grill, I flatten the bird, a method known as spatchcocking. Ask your butcher to do this for you, or learn to do it yourself following the instructions below. You can often buy your birds tunnel-boned, which means the only bones left in the bird are in the wings and legs. This makes spatchcocking much easier. Serve with a Tomato Salad (page 69) or a Tanoreen Green Salad (page 76).

Place the quail in a large high-sided dish or pan.

In the bowl of a food processor, combine the lemon juice, oil and barbecue sauce with the garlic, shallots, tomato, chilli, fresh coriander, cumin, ground coriander, salt and pepper. Process until the mixture forms a slightly chunky marinade. Pour the marinade over the quail, cover and refrigerate for at least 2 hours or overnight.

Prepare a gas or charcoal grill (or preheat the grill on your oven); it should be moderately hot. Grilling in batches if necessary, place the quail, breast-side up, on the grill, cover and cook for 5 minutes. Turn the quail over and grill the breast-side with the cover off for a further 2 minutes or until the juices run clear when the thickest part of the bird is pierced with a knife. Serve warm.

SERVES 6–9

18 quail, spatchcocked (see below),
    rinsed and patted dry
375ml fresh lemon juice
250ml extra virgin olive oil
2 tablespoons barbecue sauce
10 garlic cloves, finely chopped
4 shallots, diced
1 large plum tomato, chopped
1 green chilli, finely chopped
2 tablespoons chopped fresh coriander
1 tablespoon ground cumin
1 tablespoon ground coriander
1 tablespoon sea salt
4¾ teaspoons freshly ground black pepper

HOW TO SPATCHCOCK A QUAIL

Place the quail, breast-side down, on a clean work surface. Using sturdy kitchen scissors, snip down the skin along each side of the backbone. Pull out the backbone and discard. Turn the quail breast-side up and press down firmly on the breastbone to flatten it.

Alternatively, place the quail, breast-side up, on a clean work surface. Insert your heaviest chopping knife into the cavity of the bird from the back end to the neck. Press down firmly alongside the backbone, one side at a time, to cut it away. Discard the backbone. Press down firmly on the breastbone to flatten the quail.

STUFFED ARTICHOKES WITH MEAT AND PINE NUTS

Nobody in Nazareth prepared artichokes this way; my mother brought the idea back from a long weekend away in a nearby town. When I arrived in the States, I found that my Syrian friends had long been making stuffed artichokes with spiced meat and pine nuts – and I realised just how much my mother's cooking was influenced by neighbouring nations. My father would buy a box of fresh artichokes for my mother, who would spend the afternoon peeling and cleaning the large, spiky vegetables in order to stuff them. I loved to help her. Using frozen artichokes is much faster – and a perfectly acceptable way to make this dish. The heart will have a slightly different texture but it is still delicious! Serve with Rice and Vermicelli Pilaf (page 182).

Clean the fresh artichokes, if using (see opposite page). Preheat the oven to 230°C/gas mark 8.

Place the vegetable oil in a large frying pan over a high heat. When hot, slide the artichokes into the pan and sauté on the stem side for 3 minutes. Using tongs, turn the artichokes over and fry on the open side for 2 minutes. Transfer to a kitchen paper-lined tray, open-end down, to drain. Arrange the artichokes, stem-end down, in a large baking dish and set aside.

In a small bowl, combine the allspice, pepper, nutmeg and cardamom, if using. Place the olive oil in a medium frying pan over a medium-high heat and sauté the meat and half of the spice mixture for 8–10 minutes until the meat loses its pink colour. Add the pine nuts and almonds, the juice of 1 lemon and the salt. Stir to thoroughly combine and turn off the heat. Divide the meat mixture among the artichokes, filling them to almost overflowing and tucking in between the leaves. Reserve any remaining meat mixture.

Combine the juice of the remaining lemon and the stock with the reserved spice mixture. Drizzle this over the artichokes and pour the rest into the pan with the reserved meat mixture. Cover the pan with foil and bake for 1 hour if using fresh artichokes, 20 minutes if using frozen.

Remove the foil from the pan, reduce the heat to 150°C/gas mark 2 and bake for an additional 3–5 minutes, until the liquid has thickened. Arrange the artichokes on individual plates with the Rice and Vermicelli Pilaf. Garnish with the parsley and serve.

SERVES 8

8 (225g each) fresh artichokes or
   16–24 frozen, depending on the size
250ml vegetable oil
4½ teaspoons ground allspice
½ teaspoon freshly ground black pepper
¼ teaspoon ground nutmeg
pinch of cardamom (optional)
60ml extra virgin olive oil
1kg minced lamb from the leg,
   or minced beef
75–150g pine nuts, toasted
75–150g slivered almonds, toasted
juice of 2 lemons
1 teaspoon sea salt
1.5 litres Seasoned Chicken Stock
   (page 90)
Rice and Vermicelli Pilaf (page 182),
   for serving
chopped fresh flat-leaf parsley, for garnish

HOW TO CLEAN FRESH ARTICHOKES

1. Working with one artichoke at a time, hold it by the stem. Using kitchen shears, snip off the top 6mm or so of each leaf on the artichoke (this will get rid of the barbs).

2. Lay the artichoke on its side and, using a sharp knife, slice off the top 2.5cm or so of the artichoke to reveal the choke.

3. Slice off the stem at the base of the artichoke, taking care to keep it level so that it will sit up straight in the pan.

4. Using a melon baller, dig out the centre, including the feathery fronds, so that the centre is clean, empty and ready to be stuffed; squeeze lemon juice all over the artichoke, inside and out, to prevent it from browning. Repeat with the remaining artichokes.

STUFFED AUBERGINE OR SQUASH IN TOMATO SAUCE

◆·◆·◆

BAITINJAN AW KUSA MAHSHI

To remove the aubergine flesh – or the flesh of any soft vegetable – every Middle Eastern cook has a *manara*, a long-handled scoop designed specifically for hollowing out vegetables. Ask your butcher to mince the meat for the stuffing just once through the machine for a coarse mince.

Note: This stuffing mixture is raw, so it should be used within 24 hours of preparation. Refrigerate, covered tightly, if making in advance.

Fill a large bowl with cold water. Roll an aubergine on a clean surface until it 'gives' a bit. Using a long-handled slim spoon or apple corer, remove the flesh and discard. Drop the vegetable in the bowl of cold water and repeat with the remaining aubergines.

Place the oil in a medium frying pan and stir the allspice, pepper, cinnamon and nutmeg for 5 seconds, then sauté the meat until it begins to change colour, 4–5 minutes. Remove from the heat and add the rice, tomato, ghee or butter and salt, stirring to thoroughly coat.

Working with one vegetable at a time, fill an aubergine with the stuffing to within 2.5cm of the top of the opening (about the length of the first third of your little finger). Repeat with the rest of the aubergines, then arrange them in a 5-litre, heavy-bottomed pot or casserole so that they are standing vertically with the open-side up. Plug each opening with a piece of diced tomato. Add the puréed or chopped tomatoes to the pot followed by 250ml water and the salt and sugar. Place the pot, uncovered, over a high heat and bring to the boil. Cover and reduce the heat to medium; cook until the aubergine skins give when pierced with a fork, about 40 minutes.

Lay two or three stuffed aubergines on a plate. Slice into them lengthways to reveal the stuffing without cutting the aubergines in half, then spoon the tomato sauce on top.

VARIATION *Add 3 chopped plum tomatoes to create a colourful stuffing for aubergines, squash or vine leaves. To make stuffed cabbage, add 3 finely chopped garlic cloves.*

SERVES 6–8

16 medium Italian aubergines or 10 small aubergines, courgettes or Arabic squash (about 3kg in total) or a combination, stem ends trimmed and tops reserved
1 plum tomato, diced into 12 pieces
2kg fresh tomatoes, puréed, or 2 (400g) tins chopped tomatoes
1 teaspoon sea salt
½ teaspoon sugar

For the Meat Stuffing

120ml vegetable or extra virgin olive oil
2 tablespoons allspice
1 teaspoon freshly ground black pepper
¼ teaspoon cinnamon
¼ teaspoon nutmeg
1¼kg coarsely chopped lamb from the leg or shoulder or beef sirloin or fillet
330g short grain rice, rinsed
2 plum tomatoes or 1 beefsteak tomato, diced
6 tablespoons butter or ghee
1 tablespoon sea salt, or to taste

STUFFED AUBERGINE WITH LAMB IN LEMON SAUCE

—— ⋅•⋅ ——

BAITINJAN SHEIKH IL MAHSHI

This dish is typically served for big family celebrations but I've adjusted the recipe to serve four to six people. It takes time to prepare, but is worth every minute of effort even for a small group. My mother used to peel the skin from the aubergine every 6mm or so, so that it appeared to be vertically striped. It's a nice touch. Add a chopped jalapeño when sautéing the onions if you want to give the dish a kick.

Using a knife, open each aubergine along its length to prepare it for stuffing. Arrange in a roasting tin and set aside.

Place the oil in a large frying pan over a high heat and sauté the onions until golden, about 5 minutes. Stir in the garlic until it takes on colour, about 1 minute, then the allspice, salt, pepper, cinnamon and nutmeg until fragrant, about 30 seconds. Tip in the meat and sauté, turning occasionally, until it loses its colour, 5–10 minutes, then add the pine nuts, almonds and 2 tablespoons lemon juice and cook, stirring to thoroughly incorporate, for 1 minute. Turn off the heat.

Preheat the oven to 200°C/gas mark 6.

Divide the meat stuffing evenly among the aubergines, spooning it into the opening in each. Spread any excess stuffing over the bottom of the roasting tin and arrange the aubergines on top. In the same frying pan, combine the remaining lemon juice with the stock, tomatoes and pomegranate molasses or tamarind paste, if using, and bring to the boil. Pour the stock over the aubergines, cover with foil and bake until a fork slides easily into the aubergines, 20–30 minutes. Remove the foil and roast until the aubergines turn brown, a further 3–5 minutes.

Serve warm with the Rice and Vermicelli Pilaf on the side.

VARIATION *Stuffed Aubergine in Yogurt Sauce (Makdous Fetti)*
Prepare the Yogurt Sauce (page 138). Place a scoop of rice on a deep platter and surround it with Arabic Bread (page 57). Place the stuffed aubergine over the rice and top with the Yogurt Sauce.

SERVES 4–6

12 medium Italian aubergines (about 3kg in total), fried and peeled (page 39)
60ml extra virgin olive oil
1 medium white onion, diced
1 tablespoon finely chopped garlic
1 tablespoon ground allspice
1 teaspoon sea salt or to taste
1 teaspoon freshly ground black pepper
½ teaspoon ground cinnamon
⅓ teaspoon ground nutmeg
1.5kg chopped lamb meat from the leg or chopped beef tenderloin
75g pine nuts, toasted
75g slivered almonds
120ml fresh lemon juice
1.5 litres chicken, lamb or beef stock
2 plum tomatoes, chopped
3 tablespoons pomegranate molasses or 2 tablespoons tamarind paste (optional)
Rice and Vermicelli Pilaf (page 182), for serving

STUFFED VINE LEAVES

·•·

WARAK ANAB

I have seen friends and family eat 40–50 of these in one sitting! But that's because true stuffed vine leaves should be no bigger than a little finger. I only recently found fresh vine leaves in a produce store near the restaurant – they're at their best when they are fresh (and always delicious with Tabbouleh; page 73) but their availability is a bit random. If you do happen to find them, look for the smallest ones and be sure the surface is smooth and free of discernible fuzz. And buy extra so that you can freeze them! Of course, brined vine leaves are far easier to procure; use them if you can't find fresh.

Arrange the vine leaves in a stack, shiny-side down, with the stem end facing you. If the indentations in any particular leaf are deep, close them up by overlapping the two segments or by patching them together with pieces of another leaf. Place the reserved stems in a 5-litre pot or casserole.

Working with one vine leaf at a time, spoon 1 tablespoon of the stuffing onto the base of the leaf, just above the stem. Fold either side of the leaf over the stuffing and roll the leaf around itself to the tip, rolling tightly to keep the filling in. Place in the pot, arranging the rolls in concentric circles and layering them one on top of the other. Continue with the remaining leaves and stuffing.

Set a small, heatproof plate directly on top of the vine leaves. Pour the stock into the pot. Combine 500ml water with the salt and add to the pot. Cover the pot and bring the liquid to the boil over a high heat, then reduce the heat to medium and cook until the rice is tender and the vine leaves are soft, 1–1½ hours.

Remove the lid from the pot. Using an oven glove, hold the rolls in place with the plate while draining the liquid from the pot. Remove the plate, invert a serving platter over the pot and flip it over. Discard the vine stems. Serve the vine leaves garnished with the lemon wedges.

MAKES 100 VINE LEAVES

100 vine leaves, stems trimmed
   and reserved
Meat Stuffing (page 150)
1.25 litres stock from Seasoned Chicken
   with Stock or Seasoned Lamb with
   Stock (pages 90 or 102), or chicken stock
½ teaspoon sea salt
lemon wedges, for garnish

STUFFED VINE LEAVES AND SQUASH

KUSA WA WARAK

Kusa is squash, and *warak*, literally translated, is 'paper' – or in this case, the vine leaves. My mother made this special combination of stuffed vegetables often for Sunday supper, her only day off. We always had relatives staying at my parents' home in Nazareth and the women loved to roll the vine leaves while they caught up on the latest neighbourhood news. It is customary, in fact, for guests to do this task. It may seem like an enormous amount of food for six people, but I can say first-hand that whenever a customer orders this at the restaurant, the plate always comes back licked clean!

⚜ **COOKING TIP** Be sure to turn this out on a rimmed tray that is 10cm wider than the pot you're cooking it in.

In a small bowl, combine the allspice, salt, pepper, nutmeg and cardamom. Sprinkle the spice mixture all over the lamb chops and set aside.

Arrange the tomato slices in the bottom of a heavy-bottomed 5-litre pot or a casserole. Place the lamb chops on top, with the bones pointing to the centre and the meat around the rim, layer the squash on top and finish with the vine leaves. Add 1.25 litres water and salt to the pot. Set a heatproof plate on top of the stuffed vine leaves, pressing down firmly. Cover and bring to the boil over a high heat. Reduce the heat to low and cook until the vine leaves are tender, 40–60 minutes. Add the lemon juice to the pot and return to the boil for 2 minutes, then turn off the heat and leave to rest for 5 minutes.

Remove the lid and plate and invert a rimmed serving platter over the pot. Flip it over and serve immediately, garnished with the lemon wedges.

SERVES 6

1 teaspoon ground allspice
1 teaspoon sea salt, plus extra for the pot
½ teaspoon freshly ground black pepper
½ teaspoon ground nutmeg
pinch of ground cardamom (optional)
8 lamb chops (about 1.75kg in total), trimmed
2 plum tomatoes, sliced 6mm thick
Stuffed Squash (page 150), uncooked
Stuffed Vine Leaves (page 153), uncooked
juice of 2 lemons
lemon wedges, for garnish

STUFFED CABBAGE

MALFOOF

I know how strange this may sound, but the cabbage at home is more, well, more cabbagey than the heads I find in the States. It is partly, I suppose, because it is never watered except by the rain. Whenever I make this dish, I am reminded of the huge cabbage I once spotted in a market in Jerusalem. This cabbage was 75cm across – enough to feed more than a village! I carried it from Jerusalem to Tarshiha. When I arrived, I invited every friend and family member to come for a dinner with a menu based on that one vegetable alone! Here in the States, I have had good success stuffing white cabbage leaves. You can make the rolls a day in advance and cook them the next day and serve with a bowl of yogurt for sharing. I often pair the rolls with a favourite salad of shredded cabbage dressed in lemon juice, olive oil and garlic.

Note: This stuffing mixture is raw, so it should be used within 24 hours of preparation. Refrigerate, covered tightly, if making in advance.

Using a sharp knife, cut away the tough ribs from each boiled cabbage leaf and reserve them, stacking the leaves as you go. Place the ribs in a 5-litre heavy-bottomed pot or casserole. Arrange the lamb chops over them, then add the halved garlic heads to the pot.

Place the oil in a medium frying pan, add the allspice, pepper, cinnamon and nutmeg and stir for 5 seconds, then sauté the meat for 4–5 minutes until it begins to change colour. Remove from the heat and add the rice, ghee, garlic and salt.

Working with one cabbage leaf at a time, place it on a clean work surface with the stem end facing you. Spoon 1 tablespoon of the stuffing in the centre of the leaf. Fold either side of the leaf over the stuffing and roll the leaf up to the tip, rolling tightly to keep the filling in. Arrange the rolls in concentric circles over the lamb chops, then stack them in layers on top of each other. Place a heatproof plate directly on top of the rolls and press down firmly. Add 750ml water to the pot, turn the heat to high and bring to the boil. Reduce the heat to low and simmer until a fork inserted into the cabbage leaf doesn't resist, 40–60 minutes.

In a small bowl, combine the chopped garlic with the lemon juice. Pour the mixture into the pot, cover and return to the boil for 1 minute. Remove the pot from the heat, then take off the lid. Wearing an oven glove and holding the rolls in place with the plate, pour the liquid from the pot. Invert a serving plate over the pot and flip it over. Leave the pot on the rolls for a few minutes to allow them to settle. Remove the pot and the ribs from the top of the layers. Serve the lamb chops and cabbage rolls with lemon wedges.

BOILED CABBAGE

Fill a pot large enough to hold a single cabbage with enough water to cover and bring to the boil over a high heat. Drop the cabbage into the pot, core side up. As the cabbage boils, the core will soften. Plunge a long fork into the core; when the core is soft enough for the fork to just reach the middle of the cabbage, boil for a further 3 minutes. The cabbage should be al dente and the leaves should be separating but not mushy. Transfer to a colander to cool.

SERVES 4

2 large white cabbages (about 2¼kg each), boiled (see above)
4–6 lamb chops or pieces of lamb on the bone from the shoulder (1.25–1.5kg in total)
2 garlic heads, halved
5 garlic cloves, finely chopped
120ml fresh lemon juice
lemon wedges, for garnish

For the Hashwi Stuffing
120ml vegetable oil
3 tablespoons allspice
1 tablespoons freshly ground black pepper
⅓ teaspoon cinnamon
⅓ teaspoon nutmeg
1.25kg lamb from the leg or shoulder, coarsely chopped
330g short-grain rice, washed
40g butter or ghee
1 tablespoon crushed garlic (or a bit more if you love it!)
1 tablespoon sea salt

EGYPTIAN RICE WITH LAMB AND PINE NUTS

MANSAAF

Every region in the Middle East has its own version of this dish, which is invariably a part of every wedding feast. In Jordan, the Bedouin version is cooked with dry yogurt (which is made by boiling yogurt and removing the liquid that floats to the top; it is then strained, shaped into balls and left outside in the sun to dry completely) and rice with few, if any, spices. In Galilee, cooks make it with various spices and always nuts. It is always served on a *sidir*, which, literally translated, is Arabic for a large round tray – a symbol that there's a party going on. *Mansaaf* is the traditional stuffing for a whole roasted lamb, but that's a recipe for another cookbook! I've come to change my mind about stuffing the mixture inside the lamb – it takes away the juiciness of the meat. So I cook them separately and use the fat from the lamb in the stuffing.

In a small bowl, combine the allspice, cardamom, black pepper, nutmeg and cinnamon; set aside.

Place the vegetable oil in a large frying pan over a medium-high heat and sauté the lamb and half the spice mixture, stirring to coat the meat all over with the spices. Remove from the heat and set aside.

Place the ghee in a 5-litre casserole over a high heat. When hot, sauté the rice, stirring to coat the grains all over and until they begin to turn pearly white, 3–5 minutes. Tip in the remaining spice mixture, lamb, pine nuts, almonds and 1.5 litres boiling water. Bring to the boil, reduce the heat and simmer, covered, until the rice is cooked, 11–12 minutes. Serve warm.

VARIATION *To make an express* mansaaf, *sauté 1kg chopped boneless, skinless chicken breast in 60ml extra virgin olive oil until it loses its pink colour. Use 1.5 litres water or chicken broth in place of the stock. Proceed with the recipe as described above.*

SERVES 8–10

4¾ teaspoons ground allspice
⅓ teaspoon ground cardamom or
   3 cardamom pods, finely ground
1 teaspoon freshly ground black pepper
⅓ teaspoon ground nutmeg
⅓ teaspoon ground cinnamon
3 tablespoons vegetable oil
Seasoned Lamb with Stock (page 102),
   chicken cooled and pulled from
   the bones
60ml ghee, butter or vegetable oil
900g Egyptian rice
150g pine nuts
150g slivered almonds

KAFTA

—— •◆• ——

Kafta is common and popular across North Africa, throughout the Middle East (*kefte* or *kufta*) and in Greece (*keftedes*), Turkey, Iran, and all the way to India (*kofta*). The name, in all its variations, is derived from *kuftan*, which means 'to grind' in Persian. Every country, town, village, indeed, every cook, has a version of kafta. It is prepared in myriad ways – it can be baked, boiled, grilled, fried, steamed, poached or simply spread on a baking sheet, rolled into balls or folded into thirds over a filling like a crêpe. Many believe kafta is Turkish in origin, but Syrians from Aleppo believe they are the best at making it. If using lamb, select meat from the leg only; the shoulder is too fatty.

In a large bowl, combine the meat with the onion, tomato, parsley, pepper, salt, allspice, nutmeg and cumin, if using, and mix together with your hands. Transfer to a clean work surface and knead the mixture with your hands until smooth. Shape according to recipe instructions.

SERVES 6–8

750g each of beef and lamb, coarsely minced, or 1.5kg in total of either
1 large white onion, finely chopped
1 plum tomato, finely diced
60g chopped fresh flat-leaf parsley
1 tablespoon freshly ground black pepper
1 tablespoon sea salt or to taste
4½ teaspoons ground allspice
¼ teaspoon ground nutmeg
¼ teaspoon ground cumin (optional)

TOMATO SAUCE

—— •◆• ——

I created the very versatile tomato sauce for several dishes on the Tanoreen menu. It is wonderful for stewing okra and on the occasion when my daughter is craving pasta, I add a tablespoon of chopped basil to the sauce and ladle it over the spaghetti. It's also great for ladling over roasted chicken, meat or fish. The sauce freezes beautifully. Pour any leftover sauce into a resealable plastic bag and freeze for up to four months. Add a pinch of cumin and allspice when you reheat it; freezing can sometimes diminish the potency of spices. For a milder version, eliminate the jalapeños. You'll notice derivations of this tomato sauce are part of my Garlicky Bean and Tomato Stew (page 101) and White Bean and Beef Stew (page 106).

Place the oil in a large frying pan over a medium-high heat and sauté the shallots for 3–4 minutes. Stir in the chilli for 2 minutes, then the garlic until soft, about 1 minute, and the cumin, allspice, black pepper and salt until fragrant, 30 seconds. Add the fresh tomatoes and cook, stirring occasionally until they soften and release their juices, 4–5 minutes. Stir in the tomato purée, crushed tomatoes, sugar and 500ml water. Bring to the boil, stirring occasionally. Reduce the heat and simmer until the sauce has thickened slightly, about 10 minutes.

MAKES 1.5 LITRES (ENOUGH TO SERVE 10)

120ml extra virgin olive oil
2 shallots or 1 small white onion, finely chopped
1 long green chilli or 2 jalapeños, finely chopped
6 garlic cloves, finely chopped
1 teaspoon ground cumin
1 teaspoon ground allspice
1 teaspoon freshly ground black pepper
sea salt, to taste
4 beefsteak tomatoes or 8 plum tomatoes (about 1.5kg in total), chopped
1 tablespoon tomato purée
1 (400g) tin chopped tomatoes
1 teaspoon sugar

KAFTA WITH TAHINI SAUCE OR TOMATO SAUCE

— ◦•◦ —

KAFTA BIL TAHINA AW KAFTA BIL BANDOORA

My mother always divided the kafta and prepared half with tahini sauce and half with tomato sauce. It's a great way to enjoy both – and the extra sauce will keep in the fridge for another time. Tahini sauce is a classic topping for a tray of baked kafta; this recipe is the most common preparation all over the Middle East.

Preheat the oven to 230°C/gas mark 8. Grease a 30 x 50cm baking tray with the olive oil and set aside.

Spread the kafta meat evenly over the bottom of the baking tray, pushing it out to the edges. Using the side of your hand, make slight indentations in the meat in a grid pattern to outline eight servings. Spread 3 tablespoons olive oil all over the surface with your hands. Bake until the meat has lost its pink colour, about 20 minutes, then remove from the oven and reduce the heat to 150°C/gas mark 2 if roasting the potatoes.

If frying the potatoes, place the vegetable oil in a large, high-sided frying pan over a high heat. When hot and working in batches, if necessary, carefully slip the potatoes into the frying pan and fry, turning once, until golden brown, about 4 minutes in total. Using a slotted spoon, transfer the potatoes to kitchen paper to drain. Alternatively, brush them all over with the oil, arrange in a single layer on a baking sheet and roast in the oven until golden, about 20 minutes.

Cut the kafta along the scored markings but leave in the pan. Top with the potato slices and drizzle the tahini sauce or tomato sauce all over. Return the pan to the oven and bake for a further 5 minutes. Serve warm.

SERVES 6–8

Kafta (see opposite)
3 tablespoons extra virgin olive oil, plus
    extra for greasing and for the pan
500ml vegetable oil, for frying
3 baking potatoes, peeled, halved
    lengthways and sliced across into 6mm
    half moons
Thick Tahini Sauce (page 195) or Tomato
    Sauce (see opposite)

TANOREEN KAFTA ROLL

———— ·•· ————

Most Middle Eastern cooks make this the traditional way, with traditional tahini sauce, but I thought it could use the sweet and sour tang that comes from pomegranate molasses and a spicy kick from chilli paste. The sauce is delicious on any grilled meats, roasts and even drizzled over baked potatoes. Serve this dish alongside Rice and Vermicelli Pilaf (page 182) or roasted carrots and potatoes.

Heat 2 tablespoons oil in a large frying pan and sauté the onions until soft and golden, 8–10 minutes. Remove 2 tablespoons of the onions and set aside, then add the tomatoes and all but 2 tablespoons of the parsley, the sumac, pepper, garlic and lemon juice. Stir to thoroughly combine, then remove from the heat.

Preheat the oven to 230°C/gas mark 8. Place a 23cm square of greaseproof paper on a clean work surface. Working with 100g of kafta at a time, roll the kafta into a ball with your hands. Put the ball in your left hand (or your right hand, if you're left-handed); with the open palm of your right hand push the mixture away from you, flattening it by exerting pressure on it. Place the meat on the greaseproof paper and shape it into a 18cm round. Spoon 3 tablespoons of the stuffing down the centre of the flattened meat. Slide your hand under the greaseproof paper to fold one third of the patty onto itself and over the stuffing, then fold the opposite third over it to completely enclose the stuffing.

Transfer to a baking sheet and repeat with the remaining meat mixture and filling, making a total of 6–8 patties. Bake until cooked through and no longer pink. Drizzle the Spicy Tahini Sauce all over the patties and return to the oven for a further 3–5 minutes. Sprinkle with the toasted almonds, reserved onions and parsley. Serve warm.

SERVES 8–10

5 tablespoons extra virgin olive oil
4 medium white onions, finely chopped
3 plum tomatoes, chopped
30g chopped fresh flat-leaf parsley
1 tablespoon sumac
1 teaspoon freshly ground black pepper
1 teaspoon finely chopped garlic
juice of 1 lemon
Kafta (page 158)
Spicy Tahini Sauce (page 195)
150g slivered almonds or pine
    nuts, toasted

KIBBEH IN THE TRAY

———— ·•· ————

KIBBEH BIL SINIYAH

Named for the round pan that it is traditionally baked in, this dish is very popular throughout the Middle East, and is the way that Lebanese and Syrians typically eat kibbeh. It is lovely served with yogurt, Tomato Salad (page 69) and some olives.

Preheat the oven to 230°C/gas mark 8. Brush a 32cm-wide round-rimmed baking tray or a 4-litre baking dish with some of the oil from the hossi.

Press half the kibbeh into the tray, spreading it all the way to the edge and smoothing with your hand so that the surface is level. Spread the strained hossi mixture all over the kibbeh, making sure to cover the outer edges. Spread the remaining kibbeh over the hossi out to the edges by dipping your hands in cold water and smoothing it out. Using a knife, slice through only the top layer of the kibbeh on a diagonal, scoring it in two 1.2cm-wide sections. Bake until the meat takes on colour and is cooked through, 20–30 minutes.

Hossi (page 32), oil strained and reserved
Kibbeh (page 35)

UPSIDE-DOWN LAMB AND VEGETABLES

— ·•· —

MAKLOOBEH

When Jumana was a graduate student in Cairo, she and her roommates would often cook the national dishes from their respective countries for each other. Her Egyptian friends prepared *koshari*, a dish of lentils, rice, pasta, tomatoes and onion. Her Jordanian roommate made *Mansaaf* (page 157) that country's national dish. Jumana prepared *makloobeh*, the impressive Palestinian lamb dish meant to feed a crowd.

The exact translation of *makloobeh* in Arabic is 'upside down', because the pot, filled with layers of rice, meat and vegetables, is flipped over onto a platter. Serve with plain yogurt on the side or a Tomato Salad (page 69). Leftovers will keep, tightly covered, in the fridge for up to a week.

Place the ghee and the oil in a large frying pan over a high heat and sauté the onions until soft and golden, 7–10 minutes. Stir in the garlic cloves until they begin to take on colour, then add the rice and stir until the kernels are no longer translucent, 3–5 minutes. Add the allspice, salt, pepper, nutmeg, cumin and cardomom, if using, and stir until fragrant, about 30 seconds. Turn off the heat.

In a medium pot, bring the lamb stock to the boil.

Meanwhile, in a low, wide, heavy-bottomed 5-litre pot with a tight-fitting lid, arrange the carrot slices in concentric circles, beginning in the centre and working your way out. Layer the tomato slices on top of the carrots, then spoon the lamb on top with the aubergine and finish with the rice mixture. Add 1.5 litres lamb stock, the pomegranate molasses and the soy sauce, if using, to the pot. Cover and bring to the boil over a high heat. Reduce the heat to low and simmer until the rice has absorbed all of the liquid and is cooked through, about 30 minutes. If the rice remains undercooked, drizzle additional broth over it, 120ml at a time, until the rice is cooked to the desired texture. Turn off the heat and leave to stand, covered, for 5–10 minutes.

Remove the lid and place a serving platter 10cm wider than the pot over it. Flip the pot and gently remove it. Scatter the pine nuts and almonds over the top and serve warm.

VARIATION *From the outside, all makloobeh looks the same, but the vegetable layer leaves room for surprises – and lots of opportunity for interpretation. Some of my favourite combinations are:*

Use Seasoned Chicken with Stock (page 90) or Seasoned Beef with Stock (page 102) with 2–2.5kg roasted or fried cauliflower florets, in place of the aubergine.

Use Seasoned Lamb with Stock (page 102) with 2kg sautéed fresh fava beans or 2kg mangetout peas (add 1 teaspoon turmeric to the spice mixture when making the rice) in place of the aubergine.

SERVES 6–8

60ml ghee

80ml extra virgin olive oil

3 white onions, halved and sliced into half moons

10 garlic cloves, peeled

900g Egyptian rice

1 tablespoon ground allspice

1 tablespoon sea salt

1 teaspoon freshly ground black pepper

⅓ teaspoon ground nutmeg

½ teaspoon ground cumin

pinch of ground cardamom (optional)

2 litres stock and the meat from Seasoned Lamb with Stock (page 102), meat cut into cubes

2 carrots, sliced across on the diagonal into 6mm-thick slices

2 beefsteak tomatoes, thinly sliced across into 6mm-thick slices

4 medium aubergines, sliced across into 1.2cm-thick rounds, fried or roasted (page 39)

60ml pomegranate molasses

3 tablespoons dark soy sauce (optional)

75g pine nuts, fried

75g slivered almonds, fried

SPICED LAMB SHANK

— ◆ —

MOZZAT MHAMMARA

This is most certainly a Tanoreen dish. We rarely, if ever, prepared lamb shanks in Nazareth, because when we purchased lamb, we got the whole animal, which meant there were only four shanks for a family of seven. The meat on this part of the lamb is particularly tough – it is full of connective tissue that, when cooked over a low heat for a long time, tenderises the meat. Though the meat braises for three hours, very little of this time is active cooking time – and the meat falls right off the bone. Serve with Rice and Vermicelli Pilaf (page 182) or Basmati Vegetable Rice (page 183).

Preheat the oven to 250°C/gas mark 9. In a small bowl, combine the allspice, black pepper, cardamom, cinnamon, nutmeg and cumin. Rub half the spice mixture all over the lamb shanks.

Place 120ml oil in a large frying pan over a medium-high heat and, working in batches, sear the shanks all over, about 3–5 minutes per side. Remove the shanks to a plate. Add the onions to the frying pan and sauté until soft and golden, 3 minutes, then the remaining spice mixture and the garlic, until fragrant, about 1 minute. Stir in the basil, parsley and coriander and cook until the herbs begin to turn colour, 2–3 minutes. Add the tomatoes and sauté, stirring occasionally, until they become soft, 5–7 minutes. Stir in the lemon juice and salt and turn off the heat.

Place the potatoes, carrots and chillies, if using, in a large deep roasting tin, and brush them with the remaining oil. Roast the vegetables for 10 minutes, tossing once halfway through. Remove the pan from the oven and arrange the shanks on top of the vegetables. Using a large spoon, place a scoop of the remaining onion and spice mixture on top of each shank. Fill the tin halfway with hot water, cover the shanks with greaseproof paper and cover the tin tightly with foil. Bake for 1 hour, check the water level and fill to halfway again if some of the water has evaporated. Reduce the oven temperature to 200°C/gas mark 6 and bake for a further hour. Check the water level and add enough water to return it to its original level; bake for a final hour or until the meat falls easily off the bone.

To serve, place each lamb shank on a plate and spoon the vegetables on the side.

SERVES 6–8

2 tablespoons ground allspice

1 tablespoon freshly ground black pepper

½ teaspoon ground cardamom

½ teaspoon ground cinnamon

½ teaspoon ground nutmeg

1 teaspoon ground cumin

6 large lamb shanks, fat trimmed and discarded

250ml olive or vegetable oil

2 white onions, chopped

6 garlic cloves, finely chopped

60g chopped fresh basil

30g chopped fresh flat-leaf parsley

60g chopped fresh coriander

6 plum tomatoes or 3 beefsteak tomatoes, chopped

120ml fresh lemon juice

1 tablespoon sea salt

6 baking potatoes, peeled, halved lengthways and sliced into 6mm-thick half moons

2 carrots, halved lengthways and sliced into 6mm-thick half moons

2 chillies, deseeded and finely chopped (optional)

SMOKED WHEAT BERRIES WITH LAMB

Long considered peasant food in the Middle East, freekeh, or smoked green wheat berries, has become quite fashionable on menus not only in that region but also here in the States. Its smoky, toasted flavour is wonderfully compatible with lamb and nuts, a combination my mother used to amp up by using not just the standard almonds and pine nuts as I do here, but by scattering walnuts on top, as well. She always served freekeh with plain yogurt and a Tomato Salad (page 69). Fattoush (page 70) makes a nice accompaniment, too.

COOKING TIP I like the wheat to be al dente, like risotto, but if you prefer it slightly softer, add more stock to the pot once the initial 1.5 litres are absorbed and cook until the grains have soaked it all up.

Place the olive in a large pot over a medium heat and, when hot but not smoking, sauté the onion until softened and fragrant, 3-4 minutes. Add the garlic and sauté for a further minute., then the allspice, pepper, cardamom, if using, and nutmeg and cook, stirring, until fragrant, about 30 seconds. Tip in the freekeh and stir to thoroughly coat with the spice mixture, about 2 minutes, then add the seasoned lamb and 1.5 litres of the stock. Raise the heat to high and bring to the boil, then reduce the heat to medium and simmer for 15 minutes or until the freekeh absorbs all of the liquid. If the grains are not cooked enough to your liking, add stock 120ml at a time and cook, covered, until it is absorbed.

Spoon the freekeh and lamb mixture onto a large platter, scatter the almonds and pine nuts on top and serve.

SERVES 8

160ml extra virgin olive oil

1 white onion, diced

3-4 garlic cloves, finely chopped

1 tablespoon ground allspice

1 teaspoon freshly ground black pepper

⅓ teaspoon ground cardamom (optional)

¼ teaspoon ground nutmeg

300g freekeh (roasted and cracked green wheat berries)

Seasoned Lamb or Beef with Stock (see page 102)

75g slivered almonds, fried

30g pine nuts, fried

BAKED AUBERGINE WITH LAMB

—·•·—

SINNIYAT BAITINJAN

The Greeks have their moussaka, the Italians have their lasagne – in the Middle East we have *siniyat baitinjan.* This casserole is comfort food at its best, a great family dish and one of the most popular at Tanoreen. I have customers who have been ordering it faithfully for the last fourteen years. The key to a succulent *siniyat baitinjan* is to season it properly with the cumin and cover the meat entirely with the aubergine to prevent it from drying out. Serve it with Vermicelli and Rice Pilaf (page 182).

Place the oil in a large pot over a high heat and, when hot, sauté the onions until golden, about 3 minutes, then the garlic until fragrant, about 2 minutes. Stir in the allspice, coriander, cumin, if using, pepper, nutmeg and cinnamon until fragrant, about 30 seconds, then sauté the meat until it loses its colour, 7–10 minutes. Add the chopped tomatoes and lemon juice and cook until the tomatoes soften and release their juices, 3–5 minutes. Stir in the salt and turn off the heat. Add the pine nuts and almonds and stir until thoroughly incorporated. Set aside 1 heaped tablespoon of the meat mixture in a small bowl.

Preheat the oven to 230°C/gas mark 8. Arrange the potato slices in a single layer in a 4-litre baking dish. Spread a third of the meat mixture over the top, then have a single layer of the aubergine slices, followed by half of the remaining meat mixture. Top with a second layer of aubergine followed by the remaining meat mixture. Finish with a layer of aubergine.

In a medium bowl, combine the reserved meat mixture with the stock and the bouillon and stir until the bouillon dissolves. Drizzle the mixture all over the top of aubergine. Arrange the plum tomato slices in a single layer on top and drizzle all over with oil. Cover with foil and bake for 30 minutes. Uncover, reduce the heat to 150°C/gas mark 2 and bake until the tomatoes darken, a further 20 minutes or so. Serve warm.

VARIATION *This is a great way to transform any leftover Siniyat into a new dish altogether. Arrange whole toasted Arabic breads (page 57), on top of the tomatoes to cover. Combine 500ml yogurt with 3 chopped cloves of garlic, the juice of 1 lemon, 2 tablespoons tahini, 2 tablespoons chopped fresh mint or 1 tablespoon dried (optional); salt to taste and thoroughly mix together. Spread on top of the bread and bake at 230°C/ gas mark 8 until heated through, about 20 minutes.*

SERVES 6–8

80ml extra virgin olive oil, plus extra for drizzling

2 white onions, chopped

3 garlic cloves, finely chopped

4½ teaspoons ground allspice

1 teaspoon ground coriander

½ teaspoon ground cumin (optional)

½ teaspoon freshly ground black pepper

⅓ teaspoon ground nutmeg

¼ teaspoon ground cinnamon

1¼ to 1½kg lean beef or lamb from the leg, chopped

2 ripe beefsteak tomatoes, chopped

juice of 2 lemons

1 tablespoon sea salt

75g pine nuts, toasted

75g slivered almonds, toasted

4 baking potatoes, peeled and sliced across into 6-mm-thick slices, fried or roasted (page 107)

4 Italian (baby) aubergines (1.75–2kg in total), peeled and slice lengthways into 1.2cm-thick slices and fried or roasted (page 39)

500ml chicken, beef or lamb stock, or water

1 tablespoon powdered chicken bouillon

5 plum tomatoes, thinly sliced

BEEF-BAKED SPAGHETTI

SINNIYAT MACARONA

My mother rarely made pasta, but when she did, this was one of her go-to dishes. Back then, I much preferred the noodles with plain tomato sauce, but through the years, I have embellished her version to my own taste and love it as much as my husband always has. Unlike my mother, his mother made pasta quite often.

✣ **COOKING TIP** If using *akawi*, a soft, white salty cheese, taste it to test its saltiness. If it is too salty for your taste, boil it for 10–15 minutes and rinse under cold water. *Akawi* is available in Middle Eastern shops and some specialist markets. You can use any cheese you like, as long as it is a good melting variety.

Fill a large pot with water and add the salt and a drop of olive oil. Bring to the boil over a high heat. Add the spaghetti and cook for 7–10 minutes, until al dente. Drain and transfer the spaghetti to a 23 x 35cm baking dish.

Place 120ml olive oil in a large pot over a medium-high heat and sauté the shallots until soft and golden, about 3 minutes. Stir in the garlic until fragrant and soft, 30 seconds, then the allspice and pepper and then the bay leaves. Add the chopped tomatoes, tomato purée and stock, bring to a simmer and continue to cook for 5 minutes. Pour in the beef stock, bring to the boil and continue to cook for 3–5 minutes; the sauce will thicken slightly. Remove from the heat.

Preheat the oven to 250°C/gas mark 9. Drizzle the remaining olive oil over the spaghetti in the baking dish. Slide the spaghetti into the oven and at the same time, toast the Arabic bread for 5 minutes, tossing twice during toasting to brown evenly. Remove the spaghetti and reduce the heat to 180°C/gas mark 4. Spoon the sauce and meat over the spaghetti and toss until thoroughly incorporated. Cover with foil and bake for a further 20–30 minutes, then remove the foil and scatter the cheese on top of the spaghetti. Return to the oven and bake until the cheese is melted and golden brown, about 5 minutes. Leave to rest for at least 5 minutes to allow the casserole to firm up before cutting.

SERVES 6–8

½ teaspoon sea salt

250ml extra virgin olive oil, plus a drop for the pasta pot

1kg thick spaghetti

3 shallots, finely chopped

8 garlic cloves, finely chopped

1 tablespoon ground allspice

1 teaspoon freshly ground black pepper

5 bay leaves

2 (400g) tins chopped tomatoes

2 (200g) tubes or tins tomato purée

750ml stock and the meat from Seasoned Beef with Stock (page 102), meat cut into 2.5cm cubes

Arabic bread (page 57), for serving

750g *akawi* (not in brine), mozzarella or halloumi, grated

SIDES

STRAIGHT FROM THE EARTH

Long before I opened Tanoreen, I understood the importance – and beauty – of cooking with pure ingredients that came straight from the earth. Growing up in Nazareth, my family – in fact, most families – cooked food gathered from their own backyards. Depending on the time of year, every garden behind every home in our neighbourhood was dotted with pomegranate, lemon and tangerine trees. Almost everyone had an ample grapevine, too. My parents' garden bore enormous red tomatoes, fava beans, grassy dandelion greens, squash and cucumbers along with a tiny grove of apricot, walnut and fig trees. My mother planted her own fragrant basil, refreshing peppermint and tangy spring onions. Some of our neighbours raised goats and generously shared the fresh yogurt and cheese that they made with the milk.

If we didn't grow it and a neighbour or family member didn't either, we journeyed to the local grocer or farmers' market, where there was no such thing as processed food. Everything on offer was organic. But there were two items that we never bought: olives and olive oil. We picked, cured and pressed the olives ourselves. While my mother used these fresh ingredients in every part of the meal, she reserved the simplest preparations for the vegetable and grain side dishes that accompanied every meal.

When I moved to the States, I was determined to cook the way my mother did, with the freshest ingredients I could find. And while my backyard garden in Brooklyn is only a shadow of the one I grew up with (and without olive trees!), and the wheat harvest is a faint memory, I am lucky to live in an area in which I have easy access to farmers' markets, organic produce stores and artisanal food purveyors. Nothing takes me back home quite like a visit to the farmers' market, where the runner beans, dandelion greens, kale, okra and tomatoes – to name a few of the vegetables I cook so very often – conjure up memories of the pride my mother took in making delicious dishes from such humble vegetables. I have found top-quality grains – bulgur, cracked wheat, jasmine and basmati rices – that mean preparing classic Middle Eastern side dishes such as *Mujadara* (Lentils with Bulgur; page 178), *Shulbato* (Cracked Wheat in Tomato Sauce; page 180), and Jasmine Rice with Pine Nuts and Raisins (page 182) gives me as much pleasure as I know it once gave my mother.

'MY PARENTS' GARDEN BORE ENORMOUS RED TOMATOES, FAVA BEANS, GRASSY DANDELION GREENS, SQUASH AND CUCUMBERS ALONG WITH A TINY GROVE OF APRICOT, WALNUT AND FIG TREES.'

SAUTÉED RUNNER BEANS

•◆•

FASOOLIYA BI ZEIT

When I was growing up, runner beans and tomatoes were ubiquitous in the Palestinian cook's garden. I could always count on this dish on our Friday night dinner table; sometimes we ate it with rice as a main course and other times it was a side dish accompanied by Arabic bread. These days, I serve it as part of a mezze spread, too.

⊹ COOKING TIP The sautéed beans will keep, tightly covered, in the fridge for up to 5 days. This recipe can also be halved.

Heat the oil in a large sauté pan over a high heat. When hot but not smoking, sauté the shallots until soft and fragrant, about 3 minutes, then stir in the garlic until golden, a further 3 minutes.

In a small dish, combine the coriander, black pepper and allspice. Stir the spice mixture into the pan until fragrant, about 30 seconds. Add the runner beans and salt and stir to combine. Reduce the heat to medium, cover and cook until the beans are tender, about 10 minutes. Tip in the plum tomatoes, cover and cook until the tomatoes begin to soften, 4–5 minutes. Add the chopped tomatoes and lemon juice and cook for a further 3–5 minutes. Stir in the *teklai* and serve hot.

SERVES 8–10

250ml extra virgin olive oil
2 shallots, diced
10 garlic cloves, finely chopped
2 heaped tablespoons ground coriander
1½ teaspoons freshly ground black pepper
1–1½ teaspoons ground allspice
2.5kg runner beans, both ends trimmed, cut into 4cm pieces
1 tablespoon sea salt, or to taste
6 plum tomatoes, chopped, with their juices
1 (400g) tin chopped tomatoes
juice of ½ lemon
1 tablespoon *Teklai* (page 196)

MAKE IT A MAIN

To make a beef or lamb stew, prepare the Seasoned Beef or Lamb with Stock (page 102). After adding and cooking the chopped tomatoes and lemon juice, add 500ml of the beef or lamb stock plus the meat to the pan, raise the heat to high, cover and bring to the boil. Cook for 3 minutes. Uncover and cook for a further 10 minutes to allow the stew to thicken slightly. Stir in the *teklai* and remove from the heat. Serve hot.

SAUTÉED DANDELION GREENS WITH CARAMELISED ONIONS

—— ◦ ——

HENDBEH

Back home, dandelion greens were considered weeds by most – too bitter and tough to be edible – unless you were among the older peasant women who went up to the mountains in June and July to collect them by the bagful. When they brought the greens home, these women always prepared them simply, with sautéed onions and olive oil, and ate them with Arabic bread. Personally, I feel great when I eat dandelion greens – they just *taste* healthy, especially with a squeeze of lemon juice. Delicious. When I began making this dish at Tanoreen, my older Italian customers were in awe; they routinely ate the greens in the old country but had a hard time finding them in the States. Now they're available at farmers' markets and specialist shops.

Bring 3 litres of water to the boil in a large stockpot over a high heat. Add the dandelion greens and cook until tender, 5–10 minutes. Transfer to a colander to drain. When cool enough to handle, squeeze the excess water from the greens with your hands.

Place the oil in a large frying pan over a medium-high heat. When hot, sauté the onions until golden brown, about 2 minutes. Using a slotted spoon, transfer the onions to a plate and set aside. Add the dandelion greens to the same frying pan in batches, stirring after each addition, and sauté for 7–10 minutes. Season with the salt and pepper.

Transfer the greens to a serving platter. Drizzle with olive oil and spoon the onions on top. Garnish with the lemon wedges and serve with Arabic bread and either black or green olives.

SERVES 4–6

500g dandelion greens, chopped
120ml extra virgin olive oil, plus extra
    for drizzling
200g white onions, thinly sliced
1 teaspoon sea salt
½ teaspoon freshly ground black pepper
lemon wedges, for garnish
Arabic Bread (page 57) and black or green
    olives, for serving

FRIED TOMATOES

— ◆ —

KALAYET BANDOORA

It may surprise you to hear that I was a very picky eater throughout my childhood. When my mother cooked a dish I didn't like, I ate fried tomatoes and chips! This was one of my favourite ways to eat tomatoes and my fondness has never waned. Serve these as an accompaniment to Whole Fried Fish (page 129) or Falafel (page 52). And, of course, I'd recommend them as a vegetarian main course with a nice chunk of Arabic bread for dipping into the sauce.

In a small bowl, combine the cumin, black pepper and salt. Sprinkle half of the spice mixture over the tomato slices.

Place the oil in a large frying pan over a medium-high heat. Working in batches, gently slip the tomato slices into the pan and fry until golden, about 2 minutes per side. Using a slotted spoon, transfer to a plate. Reduce the heat to low, add the jalapeños, if using, and sauté for 1 minute, then the garlic until soft and golden, about 1 minute. Stir in the remaining spice mixture until fragrant, about 10 seconds. Return the tomatoes with their juices to the frying pan, add the lemon juice and cook for 3–5 minutes. Serve immediately.

SERVES 4–6

1½ teaspoons ground cumin

1½ teaspoons freshly ground black pepper

1 tablespoon sea salt

6 large ripe beefsteak tomatoes, sliced into 1.2mm-thick rounds

250ml olive oil

1–2 jalapeño chillies, deseeded and thinly sliced (optional)

6 garlic cloves, finely chopped

juice of 1 lemon

KALE WITH SHALLOTS AND OLIVE OIL

— ◆ —

KHUBEZEH

I love *khubezeh*, the ubiquitous Middle Eastern green that grows wild throughout the region and I often implore friends and family travelling back from the Middle East to bring it home for me. Sadly it is unavailable in the West and so here I adapt one of the many popular *khubezeh* recipes to use kale, which makes an excellent substitute. Best eaten with a squeeze of fresh lemon juice, black Kalamata olives and fresh Arabic bread (page 57), it is delicious with a dash of Harissa (page 194) and Olive Spread (page 194), too.

Place 180ml oil in a heavy-bottomed sauté pan over a medium heat. When hot, sauté the coriander, cumin, black pepper and salt until fragrant, about 1 minute. Add the onions and cook until golden, 7–8 minutes. Remove 2 tablespoons of the mixture and set aside for garnish. Stir in the garlic and cook until fragrant, about 1 minute, then the chilli, if using. Add the kale and stir until halved in bulk, 3–5 minutes. Reduce the heat, cover and cook, stirring occasionally, until tender, 15 minutes or so.

Remove the pan from the heat, drizzle the remaining oil over the kale, cover and leave to sit until the olive oil is absorbed, 1–2 minutes. Transfer to a serving dish, pour over the lemon juice and garnish with the reserved onion mixture. Serve warm.

SERVES 6–8

250ml extra virgin olive oil

1 tablespoon ground coriander

1 scant tablespoon ground cumin

½ tablespoon freshly ground black pepper

1 tablespoon sea salt

200g white onion, chopped

½ tablespoon finely chopped garlic

1 jalapeño chilli, finely chopped (optional)

1.75–2kg chopped kale, hard stems removed

juice of 1 lemon

LENTILS WITH BULGUR

—— ◦•◦ ——

MUJADARA

You would be hard pressed to find a Palestinian storecupboard that does not include lentils and bulgur, the primary ingredients in this classic dish beloved all over the Arab world. Some cooks make it with rice, others vary the spices, but all caramelise the onions that crown this dish. I use the coarsest bulgur available, though not whole bulgur. I began adding sautéed fennel when I opened Tanoreen and I love the subtle flavour it lends this dish. Serve with Pickled Turnips and Beetroot (page 188) and olives, along with a bowl of cooling yogurt.

Place the lentils in a deep saucepan with enough cold water to cover them. Bring to the boil, reduce the heat and simmer until the lentils are just tender, 20–25 minutes. Drain and set aside.

Place the oil in a large casserole dish over a medium-high heat and sauté the onions until golden brown, about 2 minutes – do not let them burn, as the colour and flavour of the sautéed onions determines the final quality of the dish. Remove a scoopful of the golden brown onions and set aside for garnish.

Add the allspice, black pepper, cumin, cinnamon and nutmeg to the pot and cook, stirring, until lightly toasted, about 10 seconds. Stir in the fennel, cooking for 2 minutes, then the bulgur wheat, stirring to coat all over with the spices, for 2 minutes. Tip in the lentils and cook for a further 2 minutes, stirring to combine. Pour 1.5 litres boiling water and the salt into the pot, cover and cook on low heat for 15–20 minutes, stirring occasionally.

Serve with a garnish of the reserved golden brown onions and a drizzle of olive oil.

VARIATION *For those with gluten sensitivities, substitute Egyptian rice, or any other short-grain rice, for the bulgur wheat.*

SERVES 8

600g small brown lentils
250ml extra virgin olive oil, plus extra
   for drizzling
2 large Spanish onions, thinly sliced
1 tablespoon ground allspice
1 tablespoon freshly ground black pepper
4½ teaspoons ground cumin
¼ teaspoon ground cinnamon
¼ teaspoon grated fresh nutmeg
1 large bulb fennel (about 180g), fronds
   trimmed and bulb diced
400g coarse bulgur wheat
1 tablespoon sea salt

LUNCH UNDER THE OLIVE TREES

At the start of the annual autumn olive harvest, my family – cousins, uncles and aunts included – would venture to my mother's inherited olive groves in her hometown of Rama, a village quite famous for its bountiful, plump olives and lush olive trees. As soon as the sun was up, we set out to do the picking, timing it so that lunch coincided perfectly with the hour when the sun was at its most intense. We gathered under a clutch of trees, where my mother laid out a delicious picnic. It was always the same – a huge pot of *mujadara* – and eating that delicious lentil pilaf with the shaved fennel and frizzled onions, surrounded by the people I loved the most, is an image that is forever etched in my memory.

It may seem odd to serve such a dish for a picnic but *mujadara* was a strategic choice. It's vegetarian – vegan even – and tastes delicious at room temperature so it didn't need to be chilled or reheated. It was also quite affordable to make for a large group and, most importantly, hearty enough to fuel us for the next twelve hours of climbing trees, picking olives and carrying baskets overflowing with them.

To this day, I'll snack on a few olives with my lunch-time *mujadara* and recall those picnics on that hillside in Rama so many years ago. It fills me with nostalgia.

OKRA WITH TOMATOES

BAMYA BELZAIT

I always make this dish when small, fresh okra is available. It's the vegetarian version of a traditional okra recipe prepared with lamb, and just as good.

If using fried okra, leave the frying oil in the pan and sauté the shallots until golden. If using roasted okra, heat 2 tablespoons of oil in a sauté pan over a medium-high heat and sauté the shallots until golden, 4–5 minutes. Using a slotted spoon, transfer to a plate and set aside.

Discard the oil, return the pan to a high heat and add the remaining 120ml oil. Stir in the garlic until fragrant and golden, about 1 minute, then the ground coriander, 10–15 seconds. Add the salt, black pepper and cumin and cook for just 2 seconds, then tip in the fresh coriander and stir for 1 minute.

Add the chopped beefsteak tomatoes to the pan, reduce the heat to low and cook until they break up and release their juices to form a sauce, 8–10 minutes. Tip in the tinned tomatoes and lemon juice and bring to the boil, stirring, for 2–3 minutes. Add the okra, reduce the heat to low and simmer until the okra is tender, about 20 minutes, taking care not to let the tomatoes stick to the bottom of the pan.

Transfer to a large platter and garnish with the fried shallots. Serve with Arabic bread.

SERVES 4–6

1kg fresh baby okra, fried or roasted (page 109)
120ml extra virgin olive oil, plus 2 tablespoons if using roasted okra
2 shallots, thinly sliced
2 tablespoons finely chopped garlic
1½ tablespoons ground coriander
1 teaspoon sea salt
1 teaspoon freshly ground black pepper
½ teaspoon ground cumin
3 tablespoons chopped fresh coriander
800g beefsteak tomatoes, chopped
4 tablespoons tinned chopped tomatoes
60ml fresh lemon juice
Arabic bread (page 57), for serving

CRACKED WHEAT IN TOMATO SAUCE

SHULBATO

My childhood summers in my father's native village of Tarshiha are synonymous with *shulbato*, a delicious, healthy bulgur pilaf that was made with the first wheat harvest. Whatever vegetables were ripe in the garden went into this. It is, perhaps, my favourite simple meal. Serve with black or green olives.

Place 180ml oil in a large frying pan over a medium-high heat. When hot, sauté the onions until golden brown, about 5 minutes. Add the cumin, salt and black pepper, then the bulgur and stir until coated all over. Tip in the tomatoes and cook until they release their juices, about 3 minutes. Stir in the tomato purée and cook for 1 minute. Add 1.5 litres water, the chickpeas and half of the roasted vegetables and bring to the boil. Reduce the heat, cover and simmer, stirring occasionally, for 15 minutes.

Transfer to a serving dish, top with the remaining roasted vegetables, drizzle with the remaining olive oil and serve hot, cold or at room temperature.

VARIATION *At Tanoreen, I fill Arabic bread with shulbato and Olive Spread (page 194) and offer it as a vegetarian sandwich.*

SERVES 4–6

250ml extra virgin olive oil
2 white onions, diced
1 tablespoon ground cumin
1 tablespoon sea salt
1 tablespoon freshly ground black pepper
600g bulgur wheat
4 plum tomatoes, diced
350g tomato purée
1 (400g) tin chickpeas, drained and rinsed
3 squash or courgettes, diced and roasted
2 chillies, chopped and roasted
1 aubergine, diced and roasted

RICE AND VERMICELLI PILAF

——— ◆◆◆ ———

When in doubt, serve any main course with this mix of rice and broken pasta strands. When my daughter, Jumana, was a young girl, she made it her main course whenever she didn't want what I was serving. Centuries ago, this was made exclusively with bulgur or smoked wheat, but when rice was introduced to the Arab world, it became a popular substitute. Egyptian rice kernels are small, round and broken; this is the only rice to use to make the authentic version of this dish. Chinese white rice is the next best thing.

SERVES 8–10

180ml extra virgin olive oil
60ml ghee or butter
500g vermicelli
800g Egyptian or Chinese rice
1 tablespoon sea salt, or to taste

Place the oil and ghee in a large saucepan over a high heat. When hot, add the vermicelli and stir until golden brown, 7–10 minutes. Stir in the rice until opaque, 3–5 minutes, then add 2–2.5 litres boiling water and salt, reduce the heat to low, cover and simmer until the rice is fluffy, about 12 minutes, stirring once halfway through.

Remove the pan from the heat, stir once more, cover and leave to stand for 5 minutes. Serve warm.

VARIATION *For those with gluten sensitivities, eliminate the vermicelli altogether along with 250ml of the water, then add another 100g of the rice.*

JASMINE RICE WITH PINE NUTS AND RAISINS

——— ◆◆◆ ———

ROZ BEL MAZAHER

This earthy, sweet and fragrant rice is a wonderful side dish with grilled meats or the Chicken Tagine (page 145). Strain the oil from the fried nuts and use it, along with the ghee or butter, to coat the rice. Sometimes I sprinkle a little cinnamon on top to add another layer of flavour.

SERVES 6

60ml vegetable oil
75g pine nuts
75g slivered almonds
60ml ghee
600g jasmine rice
1 tablespoon sea salt
1.5 litres Seasoned Chicken Stock (page 90)
   or chicken stock or water
125g sultanas
4 tablespoons orange blossom water

⚜ **INGREDIENT NOTE** Orange blossom water is an intensely floral flavouring that lends a fragrant note to all manner of Middle Eastern dishes. It is most commonly used in desserts, but I am not afraid to add a little to savoury dishes to give them another, very subtle, layer of flavour. A little orange blossom water goes a long way; it should be used with a light touch unless otherwise noted. It can be found in specialist shops, in Middle Eastern markets and online.

In a large casserole dish, combine the oil with the pine nuts and slivered almonds and fry over medium heat until golden. Transfer the nuts to a plate, add the ghee to the toasting oil in the pot and place over a medium-high heat. When hot, sauté the rice for 3–5 minutes or until the rice begins to take on colour, then add the salt, stock or water and sultanas and bring to the boil. Reduce the heat, cover and simmer for 15 minutes.

Remove the pan from the heat, uncover the pot, drizzle the orange water over the rice, cover again and leave to stand for 3 minutes. Transfer to a serving dish and top with the pine nuts and almonds.

BASMATI VEGETABLE RICE

Basmati is one of my favourite grains and is perfectly delicious eaten plain, but here I've made it a bit more special by adding whatever vegetables I could find and playing with some spices. This is the perfect side for Chicken Tagine (page 145), or any grilled meat, chicken or fish.

SERVES 4–6

120ml extra virgin olive oil
600g basmati rice
2 shallots, finely chopped
3 garlic cloves, finely chopped
1 tablespoon turmeric
1 tablespoon ground allspice
1 tablespoon ground coriander
1 tablespoon sea salt
½ teaspoon ground cardamom
½ tablespoon ground cumin
30g chopped fresh parsley
30g chopped fresh coriander
1 tablespoon finely chopped fresh sage
400g fresh or frozen petit pois
2 medium carrots, peeled and diced
3 plum tomatoes, diced
1 stick of celery, chopped
1 chilli, finely chopped (optional)
1 litre Seasoned Chicken Stock (page 90) or water

Place 60ml oil in a large casserole dish over a medium-high heat. Add the rice, stir to coat and sauté, stirring constantly, until the rice begins to take on colour, 3–5 minutes. Remove from the heat and stir in the remaining oil.

Return the casserole dish to a medium-high heat, add the shallots and sauté for 3 minutes, stirring every 30 seconds. Stir in the garlic for 1 minute, then the turmeric, allspice, coriander, salt, cardamom and cumin and cook until fragrant, 30 seconds. Add the parsley, coriander and sage, and stir for a minute, then tip in the peas, carrots, tomatoes, celery and chilli, if using, and sauté, until softened, 3–5 minutes. Carefully add 120ml stock; the liquid may spatter. Pour in the remaining stock, bring to the boil, reduce the heat, cover and simmer until the liquid is absorbed, 12–15 minutes, stirring once. Serve warm.

SPICY RICE

Spicy rice is a delicious companion to fish or prawns or any grilled meat but it can also stand alone as a vegetarian meal. I prefer using short-grain rice such as Egyptian or basmati for this dish, but any rice works. I also always make more than I need; it tastes great reheated the day after it's made.

SERVES 8–10

12 plum tomatoes, chopped
2–3 medium shallots, chopped
6 garlic cloves, chopped
4 spring onions, green and white parts, chopped
2 jalapeño chillies, chopped
60g fresh coriander, chopped
3 tablespoons fresh lemon juice
sea salt, to taste
1 litre stock from Seasoned Chicken with Stock
   (page 90) or chicken or vegetable stock or water
250ml extra virgin olive oil
1.2kg rice
1 tablespoon ground cumin
1 tablespoon ground coriander
1 tablespoon freshly ground black pepper
500g fresh or frozen petit pois (optional)

In the bowl of a food processor, combine the tomatoes with half the shallots, half the garlic, the spring onions, chillies, coriander, lemon juice and salt; process until puréed. Measure and add enough stock or water to bring the total to 2.25 litres (2.5 litres if using basmati). Transfer to a large saucepan and bring to the boil over high heat.

Meanwhile, place the oil in a large casserole dish over a medium-high heat and sauté the remaining shallots until softened, 3 minutes. Stir in the remaining garlic for 1 minute, then tip in the rice, cumin, coriander and black pepper, stirring to coat the rice with the oil until the rice begins to turn white, about 3 minutes. Add the sweet peas, if using, then gradually stir in the hot tomato purée. Reduce the heat, cover and simmer for 12–15 minutes. Serve warm.

PICKLES & SAUCES

SNACKS WITH BITE AND SAUCES WITH SPICE

A Middle Eastern meal is not a meal without a small dish of mouth-puckering pickled vegetables and a sauce served somewhere along the way.

Pickles are as essential to breakfast, lunch and dinner as Arabic bread. Briny chunks of cauliflower, carrots, chillies and turnips, to name a few, provide a wonderful, tangy counterpoint to fried falafel sandwiches, hearty stews, hummus or *foul*.

Growing up, pickle making was a yearly end-of-summer ritual for us. It would take an entire day and the preparations engaged the entire family. My father seemed to have a supernatural ability to pick the freshest, smallest, least expensive vegetables in the market, so that job fell to him. He came home with boxes piled high with cucumbers, baby aubergines, cauliflowers, peppers, turnips, beetroot, carrots and huge bunches of dill and my mother set to work chopping on the big, worn wooden board that came to symbolise the pickling season. She chopped for hours, the knife blade hitting the wood over and over, sounding a curiously soothing beat.

Before we knew it, my mother had chopped turnips into half-moons, beetroot into slivers, jalapeños into thin rings and garlic into slices. She used her hands to break up the cauliflower into florets and tossed them with chunks of carrots, then doused the mix with spicy, salty *amba*, a curry-like mango paste. I especially loved the baby cucumbers packed in vinegar and fresh dill. There were also black olives cured in olive oil and purslane and green olives spiced with chilli paste. When it was time to package them, we all got in on the act, sweeping the vegetables from the counter into metal tins, then adding the white vinegar, salt and herbs. After all the tins were filled to the brim, my father fitted the lids on, welding them shut for winter storage, and lugged them onto the roof. We opened the tins throughout the year as needed. And need them we did – we ate them at every meal.

My passion for pickles was fostered in Nazareth and only became more intense when I moved to New York. I love anything with a bite and these days, my idea of the perfect snack is a peeled lemon, cut into wedges, and liberally sprinkled with sea salt. I make all of the pickles served at Tanoreen, and while we don't store them on the restaurant's roof, the method is exactly the same as the one my mother

'MY FATHER SEEMED TO HAVE A SUPERNATURAL ABILITY TO PICK THE FRESHEST, SMALLEST, LEAST EXPENSIVE VEGETABLES IN THE MARKET, SO THAT JOB FELL TO HIM.'

used. For most of the recipes in this chapter, there is a week's wait before the pickles are ready. To reduce it to three days, boil the vinegar before adding it to the jars.

Almost every Middle Eastern dish benefits from the addition of a sauce. Indeed, there is almost no stew that can't be enhanced by a spoonful of the garlicky spice mixture known as *Teklai* (page 196). When it is stirred into boiling hot broth, it makes a very satisfying swooshing sound, a signal that the intense flavours of coriander and garlic have been released into the broth. A few dashes of Harissa (page 194), the homemade hot sauce found in every Middle Eastern pantry, can transform a dish; it is a wonderful way to amp up a vegetable dish or impart a bit of heat to a mellow stew. Some of the sauces on the following pages might be better described as spreads, among them Olive Spread (page 194), and Tomato

and Dill Spread (page 196), both of which are terrific brushed on bread before the fillings are added to a sandwich.

Of course, no proper Middle Eastern storecupboard is complete without Thick Tahini Sauce (page 195), a tangy blend of sesame paste, garlic and lemon juice. It is drizzled on Cauliflower Salad (page 75) and Brussels Sprouts with Panko (page 45) and used in all manner of meat and chicken dishes. But its most important role is as a primary ingredient in Hummus (page 36) and Baba Ghanouj (page 40), the two most popular dips in the Middle Eastern repertoire.

You'll find a pesto here, too, because I became hooked on it the minute I first tasted it upon arriving in New York. In fact, Basil Pesto (page 191), is the recipe in this chapter that best describes the journey I've taken; I serve it as a dip with *Sambosek* (page 60), stir it into tagines and use it as a marinade for chicken.

PICKLED TURNIPS AND BEETROOT

·◆·

LEFET MAKBOUS

I consider pickles the perfect snack, as my palate has always veered more towards pungent, salty foods than any other, and for me, no pickled combination is more appealing than turnip and beetroot, a marriage of sweet and hot flavours. I suppose I believe others love them as much as I do, as I serve them at every table at Tanoreen. The original recipe for these is quite basic, so I've given mine the Tanoreen 'touch' by adding jalapeños to the mix.

In a 2-litre sterilised jar with a tight-fitting lid, combine the turnips, beetroot, jalapeños, garlic and citric acid. Fill a third of the jar with vinegar and 2 tablespoons of salt. Top up the jar with water in 250ml portions. For each 250ml water added, add 1 tablespoon of salt. Cover tightly and set aside at room temperature, not to exceed 24°C, for at least 5 days. Refrigerate after opening and keep for up to 3 months.

MAKES 2 LITRES

10 turnips, cut into 6mm–1.2cm-
  thick matchsticks
2 beetroots, cut into 6mm–1.2cm-
  thick matchsticks
2 jalapeño chillies, deseeded (optional)
  and thinly sliced
2 garlic cloves, thinly sliced
1 teaspoon citric acid
distilled white vinegar and sea salt,
  for pickling

PICKLED CAULIFLOWER AND CARROTS

·◆·

ZAHRA MAKBOUSEH

I always thought that my aunt made the best pickled cauliflower until I tasted some at Khazen, a tiny but famous shwarma stand in Haifa. Today, the stand has expanded many times over, but I prefer to remember it as the place we always stopped to eat shwarma sandwiches, generously topped with briny golden pickled cauliflower, before heading for a swim in the glorious Mediterranean. It didn't get any better than that.

In a 1-litre sterilised jar with a tight-fitting lid, combine all the ingredients except the vinegar and salt. Fill a third of the jar with the vinegar and add 2 tablespoons salt. Fill the jar to the top with water in 250ml portions. For each 250ml water added, add 1 tablespoon salt. Cover tightly and set aside at room temperature, not to exceed 24°C, for at least 5 days. Refrigerate after opening and keep for up to 3 months.

MAKES 1 LITRE

1 head cauliflower, florets and stem
  cut into small pieces
1 large carrot, peeled, quartered and
  cut into matchsticks
1 chilli, deseeded and thinly
  sliced (optional)
2 garlic cloves, sliced
2 stems fresh dill, chopped
1 tablespoon coriander seeds
1 tablespoon citric acid
1 teaspoon turmeric
½ teaspoon curry powder (optional)
distilled white vinegar and sea salt,
  for pickling

❖ OLIVES, LEMONS & ZA'ATAR ❖

PICKLED JALAPEÑOS AND CARROTS

Recently, I pickled this spicy combination in the morning and they were ready to serve for a party at the restaurant three hours later. They were a big hit and no one could believe that they had been made in a few hours!

In a medium saucepan, combine the vinegar and 250ml water with the salt, dill and oregano and bring to the boil. Drop the jalapeño, carrots and garlic into the pot and return to the boil. Remove the pan from the heat and set aside to cool.

Transfer to a 1-litre sterilised jar with a tight-fitting lid. Pour the oil into the jar and seal tightly. Refrigerate after opening and keep for up to 3 months.

MAKES 1 LITRE

250ml distilled white vinegar
2 tablespoons sea salt
2 stems fresh dill
2 stems fresh oregano
18 jalapeño chillies, sliced to
    desired thickness
2 large carrots, peeled and sliced to
    desired thickness
1 garlic clove, smashed
60ml extra virgin olive oil

PICKLED STUFFED PEPPERS

FILFIL MAHSHI MAKBOUS

I don't know of any other Galilean home cook who stuffed peppers the way my mother did. When she put these on the table, they would disappear in seconds. Get creative with the stuffing here if you like; I typically use whatever is fresh and crisp at the farmer's market.

Remove the stem end of each pepper about 6mm beyond the stem and reserve. Using a spoon, remove the seeds.

In a medium bowl, combine the celery, carrots, tomatoes, cucumbers, cabbage, jalapeños and 4 tablespoons vinegar and mix together.

Spoon the stuffing into the peppers, dividing it evenly among them. Replace the stem tops on the peppers and arrange, stem-end up and stacked on top of each other, in a 4-litre jar with a tight-fitting lid. Fill a third of the jar with vinegar and 2 tablespoons salt. Fill the jar to the top with water in 250ml portions. For each 250ml water added, add 1 tablespoon salt. Add the citric acid, cover tightly and set aside at room temperature, not to exceed 24°C, for at least 5 days. Refrigerate after opening and keep for up to 3 months. To serve, cut each pepper into quarters, lengthways.

MAKES 6 PICKLED PEPPERS (ENOUGH TO SERVE 24)

6 peppers, any colour
distilled white vinegar and sea salt,
    for pickling
1 tablespoon citric acid

For the Stuffing
2 celery sticks, chopped
2 carrots, peeled and diced
2 green tomatoes, chopped
2 Persian cucumbers, diced
200g shredded white cabbage
2 jalapeño chillies, deseeded (optional)
    and diced
2 tablespoons garlic, finely chopped

PICKLED AUBERGINE IN OLIVE OIL

————— •‑• —————

BATINJAN MAKBOUS

Magic happens when aubergine stuffed with chilli paste and garlic is cured in olive oil. The aubergine softens, the chilli paste mellows and the garlic pops. Note that this version of stuffed aubergine is different from the richer, walnut-stuffed *Makdous* (page 46) – it's lighter and plays the role of condiment, making a wonderful addition to a falafel sandwich or to serve spooned next to almost any main course. Growing up, many families couldn't afford walnuts in quantity, so this is what was on offer during the week.

Bring a large saucepan of water to the boil. Slide the aubergine into the water and cook until fork-tender but not mushy, about 10 minutes. Transfer to a colander to drain and cool. Once cool enough to handle, make a 4cm incision lengthways down the middle of each aubergine. Do not cut all the way through.

In a small bowl, combine the salt and citric acid. Rub half of the salt mixture around the outside of the incisions in the aubergines. Set the aubergines aside in a colander for a further 2 hours to drain of moisture. Meanwhile, combine the chillies, garlic and chilli paste with the remaining salt mixture.

Stuff 1 teaspoon of the chilli mixture into each incision in the drained aubergines, then stack them, one on top of the other, in a 4-litre sterilised jar with a tight-fitting lid. Pour the oil over them to cover completely, adding more if necessary. Refrigerate after opening and keep for up to 3 months.

VARIATION *For vinegar-packed aubergine, follow the steps below after placing the stuffed aubergines in the jar.*

Fill the jar a third full with distilled white vinegar. Fill to the top with water, adding in 250ml portions. For every 250ml water added, add 1 tablespoon sea salt. Cover tightly and set aside at room temperature, not to exceed 24°C, for at least 5 days. Refrigerate after opening and keep for up to 3 months.

MAKES 12 PICKLES (ENOUGH TO SERVE 12)

12 baby aubergines, about 2kg
3 tablespoons sea salt
1 teaspoon citric acid
2 green chillies, such as jalapeños, finely chopped
3 tablespoons chopped garlic
3 tablespoons seedless Middle Eastern or Turkish chilli paste
500ml extra virgin olive oil, plus extra, if necessary, to cover

BASIL PESTO

— ◦•◦ —

The first time I ever tasted pesto, I was hooked. I remember the first meal I made using it like it was yesterday – linguini tossed with pesto, topped with fried aubergine and served with fresh home-baked bread. When I use pesto this way, as a sauce, I generally make it with pine nuts. If I'm going to incorporate it into a dish, I use almonds, which are less expensive.

Put the garlic in the bowl of a food processor and pulse until coarsely chopped. Add the nuts, Parmigiano-Reggiano cheese, if using, pepper and salt and chop until the nuts are finely crushed, about 1 minute. Follow with the basil, oil and lemon juice and pulse for a further minute, until smooth. Stir in red chilli flakes, if using.

To store, transfer the pesto to a sterilised jar with a tight-fitting lid. Pour a thin layer of olive oil on top of the pesto, seal and refrigerate up to 10 days or freeze for up to 3 months.

MAKES 500ML

3–5 garlic cloves
150g pine nuts, slivered almonds or
   walnut halves
2 tablespoons grated Parmigiano-
   Reggiano cheese, or to taste (optional)
1 teaspoon freshly ground black pepper
½ teaspoon fine sea salt
300g chopped fresh basil leaves
120ml extra virgin olive oil, plus extra
   for storage
juice of 2 lemons
crushed red chilli flakes, to taste (optional)

GARLIC SAUCE

— ◦•◦ —

THOUM

This is the sauce that is traditionally used on kebabs or roasted chicken. I know some people who refuse to eat either without it! The key to making a beautiful, smooth sauce is to drizzle the oil into the mixture very slowly in a thin stream. The slower you drizzle, the silkier it will be.

Place the garlic in a blender and chop until the machine won't chop anymore. With the blender running, add the vinegar, egg whites, salt and lemon salt through the opening in the top of the lid. Blend until the garlic mixture is extremely fine. Drizzle the oil, a few drops at a time, through the opening – this may take 5–10 minutes. Continue blending until the sauce is thick and silky; it should have the consistency of thick cream. The sauce will keep, in a tightly covered container, for up to 1 week in the fridge.

MAKES 500ML

40 garlic cloves
3 tablespoons distilled white vinegar
2 medium egg whites
1 teaspoon lemon salt 1 teaspoon sea salt
375ml vegetable oil

HOMEMADE HOT SAUCE

—— •·• ——

HARISSA

There's nothing quite like a homemade batch of hot sauce. Back in Nazareth, we dried our own red chillies, then soaked, drained, chopped and froze them in small batches. My sister still sends me the special peppers from Nazareth, since I've had no luck finding them in the States. Here, I prefer Middle Eastern chilli pastes to all others; the Turkish seedless brands are fantastic. You can find them in Middle Eastern shops or online. Serve this hot sauce with fish or stirred into any one of my lentil soups.

Heat the oil in a saucepan over a medium heat until hot. Add the garlic and cook until golden brown, 2–3 minutes. Stir in the chilli paste, cumin, caraway, dill and black pepper and cook, stirring, for 2 minutes. Pour in the lemon juice and 80–160ml water, depending on the desired consistency, and bring to the boil for 2–3 minutes.

Remove the pan from the heat, leave to cool and season with salt. Transfer to a jar with a tight-fitting lid. The hot sauce will keep, refrigerated, for up to 1 month.

MAKES 550ML

6 tablespoons extra virgin olive oil
6 garlic cloves, finely chopped
500ml chilli paste
1 teaspoon ground cumin
½ teaspoon ground caraway
    seeds (optional)
½ teaspoon ground dill seeds (optional)
½ teaspoon freshly ground black pepper
160ml fresh lemon juice
sea salt

OLIVE SPREAD

—— •·• ——

This is wonderful to have to hand for all manner of occasions. It is a delicious spread for almost any kind of sandwich, especially on Arabic bread stuffed with *Shulbato* (page 180); see the variation. I prefer a smooth spread, but the beauty of preparing this yourself is that you can make it whatever texture you like. For a milder spread, replace 100g of the pitted Kalamata olives with tinned pitted black olives, drained.

In the bowl of a food processor, combine all the ingredients and purée to the desired consistency. Transfer to a jar with a tight-fitting lid. The olive spread will keep, refrigerated, for up to 2 months.

MAKES 500ML

200g pitted black Kalamata olives
2 garlic cloves, chopped
1 shallot, chopped
6 capers in brine, rinsed and drained
5 sun-dried tomatoes in extra virgin olive
    oil, chopped (optional)
4 anchovies, thoroughly rinsed of
    salt, chopped (optional)
juice of 1½–2 lemons
60ml extra virgin olive oil
½ teaspoon ground cumin
½ teaspoon freshly ground black pepper

THICK TAHINI SAUCE

Tahini sauce, a smooth blend of toasted sesame paste, lemon juice, garlic and olive oil, is ubiquitous in Middle Eastern kitchens. It is *the* condiment. There is hardly a dish that isn't enhanced by it – drizzled on Falafel sandwiches (page 52) and over Brussels Sprouts with Panko (page 45); blended with puréed chickpeas for Hummus (page 36) and with charred aubergine for Baba Ghanouj (page 40). My favourite Whole Fried Fish (page 129) is served with the sauce mixed with parsley. At Tanoreen, I mix it into salad dressings and drizzle it into cauliflower casseroles. My daughter? She dips chips in it! Learn to make this and you will have a simple, delicious, versatile sauce to add to your repertoire.

In the bowl of a food processor, combine the tahini, garlic, lemon juice and salt and process on a low speed for 2 minutes or until thoroughly incorporated. Turn the speed to high and blend until the tahini mixture begins to whiten. Gradually add up to 120ml water until the mixture reaches the desired consistency.

Transfer the sauce to a serving bowl and garnish with the parsley. Leftover sauce can be stored, tightly covered in the fridge, for up to 2 weeks.

VARIATIONS

Spicy Tahini Sauce Add 60ml pomegranate molasses and 2 tablespoons chilli paste to the bowl of the food processor and pulse until thoroughly incorporated.

Sandwich Sauce To make a thinner version for drizzling on falafel, kafta or cauliflower tagine, add water to the mixture and pulse to the desired consistency.

Fetti Sauce Combine 250ml of the tahini sauce with 250ml natural yogurt in the bowl of a food processor and pulse until smooth to make a wonderful, simple sauce for Chicken Fetti (page 138).

MAKES 625ML

375ml tahini (sesame paste)
3–4 garlic cloves, crushed
juice of 5 lemons or to taste (about 250ml)
1 teaspoon sea salt
chopped parsley, for garnish

DESSERTS

SATISFYING A SWEET TOOTH

Weekends in our Nazareth home revolved around food. Friday or Saturday were synonymous with raw kibbeh and fried fish, but Sunday morning invariably meant awakening to the unmistakable aroma of fresh baked Semolina Cake (*Harisa*; page 204). My mother would rise long before the rest of us, so that by the time we sauntered into the kitchen, she could present us with a piece of the dense, golden treat, soaked in sugar syrup infused with orange blossom and rose water. She baked the cake on a huge baking sheet, in the hope that a large batch would take us through to the following Sunday.

It only barely did, since in the Middle East, it is not unusual to eat dessert for breakfast as well as any other time of the day. Macaroni cookies (page 215), Date Cookies (*Ka'ik*; page 214) and *Mamool* Walnut Cookies (page 211), for example, are typically served with strong Turkish coffee in the morning. Flower-Scented Custard with Pistachios and Syrup (*Sahlab*; page 202), a soothing, chilled custard, is often eaten after lunch.

The hallmarks of Middle Eastern desserts are few yet distinct. Unlike any other course in a meal, the portions are generally quite small. Because they are made with such rich ingredients, a bite or two is all one needs to satisfy a sweet tooth. In the recipes that follow, you'll notice a handful of ingredients that show up in most Middle Eastern desserts. Fragrant rose and sweet orange blossom water almost always infuse the simple syrup, or *attir*, that tops desserts, such as Knafeh (page 216) as well as the dough used for Date Cookies (page 214), the poaching liquid for Stuffed Fresh Dates (page 213) and the custard in Sahlab (page 202). Nuts, too, are a primary dessert ingredient. In fact, the only other ingredient I use more than nuts at Tanoreen is parsley! If pistachios, walnuts, pine nuts or almonds are not layered, stuffed or folded into a dessert, then we sprinkle some on top for good measure. Various combinations of sweet spices – cinnamon, nutmeg and cloves – are also ubiquitous. These earthy seasonings are mixed into date and nut fillings and stirred into sugar syrup to infuse it with distinctly Middle Eastern flavours.

The combination of fragrant flower waters, nuts and spices is hard to compete with. So you will find that, more than in any other chapter in this book, I stay fairly true to traditional Middle Eastern recipes, with only a few variations and additions I have experimented with at Tanoreen.

'MY MOTHER WOULD RISE LONG BEFORE THE REST OF US, SO THAT BY THE TIME WE SAUNTERED INTO THE KITCHEN, SHE COULD PRESENT US WITH A PIECE OF THE DENSE, GOLDEN TREAT, SOAKED IN SUGAR SYRUP INFUSED WITH ORANGE BLOSSOM AND ROSE WATER.'

FLOWER-SCENTED CUSTARD WITH PISTACHIOS AND SYRUP

SAHLAB

My gluten-sensitive customers are mad for this creamy dessert, fragrant with just a hint of rose and orange blossom waters. It can be prepared as either a hot drink – in which case, I add a dash of cinnamon, some raisins and crushed walnuts – or a chilled custard topped with crushed pistachios and fragrant syrup, as I make it here.

Place the mastic and ½ teaspoon of sugar in a small bowl. Using the back of a spoon, crush the mastic to a coarse powder.

Pour the milk into a medium saucepan and stir in the mastic mixture. Warm over a medium heat until the milk comes to the boil. Stir in the cornflour mixture, rose water and orange blossom water. Using a hand mixer, mix until the liquid begins to thicken slightly and coats the back of a spoon, about 2 minutes. Transfer to a 23cm round cake tin or pour into individual serving glasses or ramekins. Leave it to cool slightly, cover with cling film and refrigerate until firm and thoroughly chilled, at least 3 hours.

If you have made a cake, invert a serving plate at least 10cm wider than the cake tin over the tin. Flip over to release the *sahlab* and the syrup that has formed on the bottom of the pan and cut into wedges. Sprinkle the top with the pistachios and serve cold.

SERVES 6–8
(ONE 23CM ROUND CUSTARD)

1 teaspoon ground mastic
185g plus ½ teaspoon sugar
2 litres cold milk
125g cornflour, mixed with 120ml water
2 tablespoons rose water (optional)
2 tablespoons orange blossom water
150g chopped pistachios

RUBY RED FRUIT COMPOTE

This raspberry and cherry sauce is very versatile – it is not only delicious over *sahlab* (above) but can brighten a scoop of ice cream or a slice of cake, too.

In a medium saucepan, combine the raspberries and cherries with the sugar, Grand Marnier, vanilla and lemon juice. Cook over a high heat until the fruit begins to break down, about 5–8 minutes. Reduce the heat to low and simmer until the mixture thickens slightly, 20–25 minutes. Remove from the heat and leave to cool before serving. The compote will keep, tightly covered, in the fridge for up to 2 weeks.

MAKES ABOUT 750ML

500g fresh or frozen raspberries
500g fresh or frozen cherries, pitted
100g brown sugar
2 tablespoons Grand Marnier liqueur
1 tablespoon vanilla extract
5 drops fresh lemon juice

COCONUT SEMOLINA CAKE

— ·•· —

HARISA

Not to be confused with the North African hot sauce with the same name, this toothsome, sweet cake is known as *namoura* or *basboosa* in some regions of the Middle East, but in Galilee, it is *harisa*. This particular version is one of my mother's most treasured recipes, perfected as only she could, by adding her own touch. In this case, it's coconut, an ingredient you'll never find in other *harisas* (omit it if you want to make the traditional version). This cake is quite simple to make, but its richness and exotic flavour make it a special dessert – and its size is perfect for a crowd. It freezes well, but the recipe can also be halved and baked in a 15 x 23cm cake tin to yield a smaller cake.

⚜ **COOKING TIP** You probably won't need all of the simple syrup called for here. But it's nice to have to hand for the next semolina cake, or to stir into iced tea or lemonade. It will keep, covered, in the fridge for up to 4 months.

Preheat the oven to 175°C/gas mark 4. In a large mixing bowl, stir together the sour cream and baking powder and leave to stand for 1 minute, or until the sour cream begins to rise. In a small bowl, stir together 4 tablespoons of the sour cream and baking powder mixture with 4 tablespoons melted butter and set aside.

In another large bowl, combine the farina with the remaining melted butter and the coconut, sugar, bicarbonate of soda and vanilla extract. Blend with a rubber spatula or your hands until thoroughly incorporated, about 5 minutes. Alternatively, combine the ingredients in the bowl of a freestanding mixer fitted with the paddle attachment and beat on medium speed until thoroughly incorporated. Add the sour cream mixture to the farina batter and mix thoroughly until the ingredients are thoroughly incorporated.

Spread half of the reserved sour cream and butter mixture in the bottom of a deep-sided 30 x 50cm baking tray. Spread the farina batter evenly over it, pushing it out to the corners with a rubber spatula, then spread the remaining sour cream and butter mixture evenly on top. Bake for approximately 30 minutes or until golden brown. While still warm, pour the simple syrup over the cake. Transfer the tray to a wire rack to allow the cake to cool to room temperature.

Cut the cake into 12 squares, garnish each piece with the pistachio nuts and serve. The cake will keep, covered with cling film, at room temperature for up to 3 days or in the fridge for up to 2 weeks. Reheat in a low oven before serving.

VARIATION *Walnut Cake With the simple addition of 450g chopped walnuts, 125g pitted, chopped dates and 3 tablespoons cocoa powder to the farina batter, you can transform the semolina cake into an entirely different dessert.*

SERVES 12
(ONE 30 X 43CM CAKE)

1 litre sour cream
2 tablespoons baking powder
350g unsalted butter, melted and cooled
800g white farina, such as Cream of
    Wheat, or fine semolina
150g dessicated coconut
185g sugar
¼ teaspoon bicarbonate of soda
3 tablespoons vanilla extract
Simple Syrup (page 216), at
    room temperature
75g chopped pistachio nuts (optional)

PUTTING BAKING POWDER TO THE TEST

Combining the sour cream with baking powder is a good method for testing the power of your baking powder. If the sour cream doesn't rise, your baking powder has exceeded its expiration date.

CHOCOLATE-RASPBERRY CAKE

I am a chocoholic, a condition I'm afraid I've passed on to my daughter, who can't resist a bite of the darkest variety every night. So it makes sense that I would occasionally offer a chocolate dessert at Tanoreen. I created this cake for a Valentine's Day menu; it was born out of a challenge I presented to myself to make the chocolatiest chocolate cake possible. After a bit of experimentation, I came up with this. The secret lies in multiple but distinct layers of chocolate flavour – dark cocoa powder, strong chocolate liqueur and dark chocolate. There's also a bit of instant coffee in the mix, an addition that imparts a certain earthiness that intensifies the chocolate flavour even more.

Preheat the oven to 175°C/gas mark 4. Dust the bottom and sides of a 30–35cm round baking tin with a thin coating of flour. Tap out the excess. Chill a medium mixing bowl and the beaters of a hand mixer or large hand whisk in the fridge.

In a medium bowl, combine the flour, baking powder and bicarbonate of soda.

In the bowl of a freestanding mixer, beat the eggs on medium speed until pale yellow, about 4 minutes. Add the sugar, olive oil, cherry juice and vanilla and beat until smooth. With the beater running, gradually add the flour mixture to the bowl and beat until the batter is smooth, about 5 minutes. With a rubber spatula, fold in the coconut, if using, the walnuts and chocolate chips.

Pour the batter into the prepared tin and bake until a skewer, inserted in the centre, comes out clean, 25–30 minutes. Let the cake cool slightly while preparing the syrup and whipped cream.

To make the syrup, bring 120ml water to the boil in a medium saucepan. Add the Grand Marnier, if using, maple syrup, ground coffee, sugar and cocoa powder and stir, using a wooden spoon, for 1 minute. Remove from the heat and set aside.

To make the whipped cream, pour the cream into the chilled bowl. Fit a hand mixer with the chilled beaters and beat the cream on medium speed until it begins to thicken. Alternatively, use a large hand whisk to beat the cream, making large strokes and changing direction every so often. Add the vanilla and sugar and continue to whisk until peaks begin to form and the desired stiffness is reached.

Run a knife around the rim of the tin to loosen the cake from the edges. Invert a large plate over the tin and flip the cake out onto it. Allow the cake to cool completely then pour the syrup over it, allowing it to soak through. Chill the cake in the fridge for at least 15 minutes before serving. Cut into wedges and serve topped with the whipped cream and the fresh berries, dusted with icing sugar.

SERVES 10–12

For the Cake
250g plain flour, plus extra for dusting the tins
4½ teaspoons baking powder
½ teaspoon bicarbonate of soda
4 medium eggs, beaten
185g caster sugar
180ml extra virgin olive oil or unsalted butter, melted
250ml cherry or raspberry juice
2 tablespoons vanilla extract
75g dessicated coconut (optional)
150g chopped walnuts
125g semisweet chocolate chips

For the Syrup
5 tablespoons Grand Marnier liqueur (optional)
3 tablespoons organic maple syrup
2 tablespoons ground instant coffee
2 tablespoons sugar
1 tablespoon unsweetened cocoa powder

For the Whipped Cream
500ml chilled double cream
1 tablespoon vanilla extract
1 tablespoon sugar

500g fresh raspberries, strawberries or blackberries
icing sugar, for dusting

FLOURLESS TANGERINE APRICOT CAKE

———— •◆• ————

As time goes on, more and more of my customers are requesting gluten-free dishes. It is easy to put together a meal with this in mind, since many of our savoury dishes are naturally free of gluten. Of course, cakes and pastries are a challenge, but one I was happy to take on. I experimented with various gluten-free alternatives to flour and found that a combination of ground almonds and pistachios result in a flour with wonderful texture. Grind the nuts in a nut grinder to a consistency similar to farina; take care not to grind them too finely or it will affect the cake's texture. This makes a lovely large cake and so is perfect for a party.

Place the tangerines in a large saucepan with enough water to cover and bring to the boil. Continue to boil until the fruit is soft, 25–35 minutes, depending on the ripeness of the fruit. Transfer to a colander to drain, then put the tangerines in a blender and purée until smooth. Alternatively, use a hand mixer to purée the tangerines.

Place the apricots in the same pan with enough water to cover and bring to the boil. Continue to boil until the fruit is soft, 15–20 minutes, depending on the ripeness of the fresh apricots or the freshness of the dried apricots. Transfer to a colander to drain, then put the apricots in a blender and purée until smooth. Alternatively, purée the apricots using a hand mixer.

Preheat the oven to 175°C/gas mark 4. Prepare a 40cm round cake tin with non-stick cooking spray.

Meanwhile, in a medium bowl, combine the sugar, almonds, pistachios, walnuts, coconut, if using, and baking powder. Set aside.

In the bowl of a freestanding mixer, beat the eggs until pale yellow. Add the puréed apricots, the Frangelico, if using, and vanilla and beat until thoroughly incorporated. With the motor running, gradually add the nut mixture to the egg mixture and mix until smooth, 3–5 minutes.

Pour the batter into the baking tin, filling to about 2.5cm below the rim as this cake does not rise much, and bake until a skewer inserted in the middle comes out clean, 35–40 minutes. Transfer the tin to a wire rack to cool slightly.

To serve, run a knife around the edge of the cake tin to loosen it. Invert a large plate over the tin and flip it over to release the cake. Serve the cake warm with whipped cream, fresh fruit or ice cream.

SERVES 10–12 SERVINGS (ONE 40CM ROUND CAKE)

8 tangerines, peeled, segmented
   and deseeded
8 apricots, peeled and pitted, or 125g dried
185g sugar
500g peeled raw almonds, ground to
   the texture of farina
150g pistachios, skinned and ground to
   the texture of farina
150g crushed walnuts
40g dessicated coconut (optional)
2 tablespoons baking powder
8 medium eggs
4 tablespoons Frangelico liqueur (optional)
2 tablespoons vanilla extract

EASTER IN NAZARETH

When I was a young girl, my uncle, who lived in the US, came to visit Nazareth for Easter after a nearly ten-year absence.

Easter tradition back in those days dictated that in the week leading up to the Sunday celebration, neighbours and family baked together during the day, then shared a lively, hearty dinner together each night at a different home. Upon his arrival, my mother greeted my uncle with a huge hug and, to his great surprise, a gaggle of women – at least ten – behind her, mixing, rolling and baking traditional Easter cookies. Some were in charge of the *mamool*, little dome-shaped sweets filled with cinnamon-spiced walnuts or pistachios, perfumed with orange blossom water and sprinkled with sugar. Others were presiding over the wreath-shaped, date-filled *ka'ik*, fragrant with cinnamon, cloves and nutmeg.

Our guest was in awe of our assembly line; we set up three stations, one for making the dough, another for making the stuffing and a third for rolling the stuffing into the dough. Clouds of flour filled the air, and the counters were piled high with semolina, nuts, sugar, vegetable fat, spices and dates. Each woman stuffed, rolled and decorated cookies by the dozen and, once a baking tin was full, called on one of her children to carry it to the village baker, since homes in those days didn't have their own ovens. Not surprisingly, the children were always standing by, eager to help... and sneak some nuts, date filling or a cookie, warm from the oven.

Why bake alone when you can bake together? Why make one batch of cookies when you can make hundreds? That is the Palestinian philosophy. Back then, Easter week was synonymous with the smell of brewed coffee and those spiced, earthy cookies. There were platters mounded high everywhere, as if dropped from heaven. And, curiously enough, the cookies were shaped in ways to make a young girl believe they just may have. *Ka'ik*, shaped in circlets for the holiday, symbolised the crown of thorns Jesus wore on the cross, and the *mamool's* domed shape was said to resemble Jesus' tomb. Sadly, these rituals and traditions have faded over time, but I'll never forget how they embodied the generosity of my community back then.

'UPON HIS ARRIVAL, MY MOTHER GREETED MY UNCLE WITH A HUGE HUG AND, TO HIS GREAT SURPRISE, A GAGGLE OF WOMEN – AT LEAST TEN – BEHIND HER, MIXING, ROLLING AND BAKING TRADITIONAL EASTER COOKIES.'

✦ OLIVES, LEMONS & ZA'ATAR ✦

MAMOOL WALNUT COOKIES

Making *mamool* by hand is in my DNA, so I forego the moulds that are now available to make the process go faster. Of course, using them will not impact on the taste of the cookie, but they will make a pretty design on top. They are available from Middle Eastern grocers and specialist kitchen shops. If you opt to use pistachios, soak them for 30 minutes, then drain them to help maintain their gorgeous green colour. If you want to go dairy-free here, you can substitute orange blossom water for the milk.

In a large bowl, combine the nuts with the butter, rose water, orange blossom water, sugar, cinnamon and cloves; stir to thoroughly coat the nuts. Set aside.

In a large bowl, combine the semolina, farina and flour. Sprinkle the mastic and mahlab over the dry ingredients. Make a well in the middle of the dry ingredients and add the yeast and sugar to the well. Add 3 tablespoons warm water to the yeast mixture and leave to sit until the yeast mixture begins to foam, about 1 minute. Add the milk and, with a fork, gradually mix the wet and dry ingredients together until a dough forms.

Transfer the dough to a clean work surface and knead until it is pillow-soft and workable. If the dough becomes too stiff to work with, gradually add water to bring it to a workable consistency. Return the dough to the bowl and set aside for 1 hour, covering the bowl with a clean tea towel to prevent the dough from drying out as you shape the cookies.

Preheat the oven to 190°C/gas mark 5. Line two baking sheets with baking parchment.

Place about 3 tablespoons of dough in the palm of one hand and use the other palm to roll it into a ball. Make an indentation in the ball with your finger. Spoon 1½ tablespoons of the nut mixture into the indentation, then bring the edges of the dough up around the filling. Pinch the edges all around to seal in the filling. Flip the cookie over into the other hand, seam-side down, and gently press until the seam side is flattened. Place the cookie on a prepared baking sheet and repeat with the remaining dough.

Bake until the cookies are pale blond, 12–15 minutes. Transfer to a wire rack to cool. The cookies can be stored at room temperature for 2 days; they will keep in an airtight container in the fridge for up to 2 weeks or in the freezer for up to 3 months. Before serving, dust liberally with icing sugar.

MAKES 3½ DOZEN COOKIES

For the Filling
1.5kg pistachios or walnuts, shelled and coarsely chopped
3 tablespoons butter, ghee or vegetable oil
3 tablespoons rose water
3 tablespoons orange blossom water
185g caster sugar
½ teaspoon ground cinnamon
pinch of ground cloves

For the Dough
1kg fine semolina flour
500g white farina
500g plain flour
1 tablespoon mastic
1 tablespoon mahlab
1 teaspoon active dry yeast
1 tablespoon sugar
500ml milk or orange blossom water
icing sugar, for dusting

ROLLED DATE COOKIES

— ◆ —

MAOROOTA

I have tried in vain to replicate the date roll my mother used to make. This is pretty close, though I believe she used more butter. These days, since we're all trying to eat more healthily, I often make it with olive oil instead of ghee, with nice results. If you do use olive oil, add 2 tablespoons of anise seeds to the dough. Serve with coffee or tea.

In a large bowl, combine the dates with the oil, cinnamon, cloves and allspice. Work with your hands until the mixture forms a paste. (If the dates are hard, first combine them with the oil in a large pan and cook over a low heat to soften. Then add the spices and work into a paste.) Set aside.

In another large bowl, whisk together the flour, yellow and white farinas, mahlab, if using, mastic and all but 1 tablespoon of the sugar. Make a well in the centre and pour in the ghee or olive oil. Using your hands, work the mixture into a dough. Cover and set aside to rest for 30 minutes–1 hour.

When the dough has finished resting, combine the remaining 1 tablespoon sugar with a drop of warm water and the yeast in a small bowl. Make another well in the centre of the dough and pour in the yeast mixture. Add the orange blossom water and work the dough from the interior of the well out for 3–5 minutes. Alternatively, put the dough in the bowl of a freestanding mixer fitted with the dough hook, make the well, add the yeast mixture and orange water and mix on medium until the dough is smooth and soft.

Shape the dough into four balls and place on a clean surface. Cover with a clean tea towel and leave to rest for about 15 minutes. Meanwhile, preheat the oven to 200°C/ gas mark 6 and grease two baking sheets with olive oil.

Dust a clean work surface with flour and roll out each ball of dough to 1.2cm thickness to make a 40cm round. Divide the date mixture among the rounds, spreading it evenly out to the edges and top each with the walnuts. Roll each round of dough up like a Swiss roll, arranging them on the prepared baking sheets at least 5cm apart.

Bake the rolls for 10 minutes, then check to see if the dough is taking on too much colour; it should be pale. Reduce the heat to 150°C/gas mark 2 and bake for 15–20 minutes. Set aside to cool.

Slice into 2.5cm-thick cookies and serve. The cookies will keep in a covered container in a cool, dry place for up to 2 weeks or for up to 3 weeks in the fridge.

VARIATIONS *To make Rolled Fig Cookies, replace the date mixture with fig preserve and use pistachios in place of the walnuts. Spread the preserve onto the dough as you would on a sandwich. For truly indulgent rolled cookies, sprinkle some grated dark chocolate onto the filling before rolling.*

MAKES 3 DOZEN COOKIES

2kg pitted fresh dates, chopped
2 tablespoons vegetable oil
½ teaspoon ground cinnamon
pinch of ground cloves
pinch of ground allspice
250g plain flour, plus more for dusting
125g fine yellow farina
125g white farina
1 teaspoon mahlab (optional)
1 teaspoon mastic
100g sugar
375ml ghee or extra virgin olive oil,
   plus more for greasing
1 tablespoon active dry yeast
375–500ml orange blossom water,
   milk or water
500g crushed walnuts

⚜ **COOKING TIP** Sometimes I parbake the roll and freeze it, then thaw and finish off the baking just before serving. To do so, bake the roll for 10–12 minutes, cool completely, then wrap tightly in cling film and freeze for up to 2 months.

STUFFED FRESH DATES

— ❖ —

Admittedly, dates fresh off the tree are not easy to find in the West, but I see them with increasing frequency at farmers' markets or from online vendors. Their season is short – just three months beginning in August – but the memory of that first bite will last forever. Fresh dates are as crisp as a Granny Smith apple, as hard and yellow as a Golden Delicious, but taste just like a date. Look for dates in the *khalal* stage of ripeness, when they are golden and a bit crunchy; it comes after the green, or *kimri*, stage and just before the *rutah*, or soft and gooey, stage. Most dates you find in the market are firm and dark, in the fourth and final stage of ripeness called *tamir*.

Stuff each date with an almond and set aside.

In a large saucepan, bring 500ml water to a simmer over a medium heat. Add the sugar, stirring until dissolved, then stir in the orange juice, Frangelico, orange blossom water, rose water, cloves and cinnamon stick. Raise the heat and bring to the boil. Stir in the lemon juice, reduce the heat and simmer for 10 minutes; the mixture will begin to thicken.

Gently slip the dates into the saucepan, taking care not to let the almonds fall out. Return to a simmer and cook for 12 minutes. Turn off the heat and leave to cool, uncovered, until the dates reach room temperature.

Transfer the dates and syrup to a heatproof container and refrigerate until completely chilled. Divide the dates among four plates and serve with a scoop of the ricotta and a drizzle of the simple syrup.

SERVES 4 (8 STUFFED DATES PER SERVING)

32 fresh *khalal* dates, stem end
    trimmed, pitted
32 raw skinless almonds or walnuts
150g sugar
60ml fresh orange juice
50ml Frangelico, Amaretto or Grand
    Marnier liqueur
1 tablespoon orange blossom water
1 tablespoon rose water
5 whole cloves
1 cinnamon stick
2 drops lemon juice
150g ricotta cheese
Simple Syrup (page 216), for drizzling

DATE COOKIES

— ⋅•⋅ —

KA'IK

You might notice that the dates you buy are a bit tough or dry in places. To soften them, place the dates in a frying pan over a very low flame and mash with a wooden spoon or spatula as they warm. If you like a sweeter cookie, you can add additional sugar to this dough. I prefer to use less since I find the dates to be sweet enough.

Put the flour in a large bowl, add the melted butter and knead with your hands until the butter is completely absorbed into the flour. Make a well in the centre of the bowl and add the yeast, sugar and 2 tablespoons hot water. Leave to sit for 1 minute. Add the mastic and mahlab to the flour mixture. Add the orange blossom water to the yeast mixture and knead it all together until it forms a soft dough. Cover with a tea towel and leave to rest for 30 minutes.

Combine the dates with the oil, rose water, cinnamon, cloves and nutmeg in a large bowl. Knead with your hands until the mixture has the consistency of a soft paste.

Preheat the oven to 190°C/gas mark 5. Line two baking sheets with baking parchment.

Place about 3 tablespoons of dough in the palm of one hand and use the other palm to roll it into a ball. Make an indentation in the ball with your finger. Spoon 1½ tablespoons of the date mixture into the indentation, then bring the edges of the dough up around the filling. Pinch the edges all around to seal in the filling. Flip the cookie over into the other hand, seam side down and gently press until the seam side is flattened. Place the cookie on the prepared baking sheet and repeat with the remaining dough.

Bake until the cookies are golden brown, 15–20 minutes. Transfer to a wire rack to cool. The cookies can be stored at room temperature for 2 days; they will keep in an airtight container in the fridge for up to 2 weeks or in the freezer for up to 3 months. Before serving, dust liberally with icing sugar.

MAKES 3½ DOZEN COOKIES

For the Dough
750g plain flour
1kg unsalted butter, melted
1 tablespoon dried yeast
1 tablespoon sugar
1 tablespoon mastic
1 tablespoon mahlab
500ml orange blossom water or
   warm milk

For the Filling
1.5kg Medjool dates, pitted
3 tablespoons corn oil, butter or ghee
2 tablespoons rose water (optional)
½ teaspoon ground cinnamon
pinch of ground cloves
pinch of ground nutmeg
icing sugar, for dusting

MACARONI COOKIES

—— •◦• ——

Around the time that the olives from our trees were first pressed, my mother invariably made these subtle, anise-flavoured cookies. She never made less than two months' worth of them – about 25 pounds of cookies! – because they store well and are wonderful to have on hand to serve with coffee or tea when unexpected guests stop by. The cookies are named for their hollow interior, like the pasta. I enjoy them dipped in cold Simple Syrup (page 216) or in melted chocolate. Lately, I've begun stuffing them with dates.

Sift the flour into a large bowl and stir in the sugar, sesame seeds and the ground and whole anise seeds. Add the oil and work it into the flour with your hands until the flour has taken on as much as it can, 3–5 minutes (there will be excess oil after kneading that you can discard). Gradually add up to 250ml cold water and mix with your hands after each addition until a dough forms. If the dough does not come together, add more water, a few teaspoons at a time, until it does.

Preheat the oven to 190°C/gas mark 5. Prepare two baking sheets with baking parchment.

To shape the cookies, pull a piece of dough the size of a ping pong ball from the batch. Place it on a flat sieve or an overturned strainer. Press it into a 5 x 8cm rectangle. Using four fingers, roll the dough from the top toward you so that it is folded onto itself. Place the cookie on a baking sheet, seam side down. Repeat with the remaining dough, spacing the cookies 2cm apart.

Bake the cookies until very lightly browned, 12–15 minutes. Leave to cool. The cookies will keep, tightly wrapped. Or wrap them in two layers of cling film, place in a resealable plastic bag and freeze for up to 2 months.

VARIATION *Lenten Macaroni Cookies* *My Mum made a spiced, date-stuffed version of this simple cookie during Lent by working ¼ teaspoon ground cinnamon and a pinch each of ground cloves and allspice into 1kg fresh pitted dates. She added 1 teaspoon of nigella seeds to the dough. To fill, flatten a walnut-sized piece of dough into a 5 x 2.5cm rectangle. Roll 2 teaspoons of the date stuffing between your palms to the same length as the dough, set it in the centre of the dough and wrap the dough up around it, pinching the seam together. Bring the ends of the dough around to meet each other to form a wreath. Bake as described above.*

MAKES 5 DOZEN COOKIES

750g plain flour

300g sugar

250g unhulled sesame seeds
(shells on)

80g ground anise seeds

80g whole anise seeds

750ml extra virgin olive oil or 500ml extra
virgin olive oil plus 250ml vegetable oil

KNAFEH

—— ••• ——

Katayfeh **is the name given to the shredded filo pastry used to make these traditional cheese- or walnut-filled desserts, which are found all over the Middle East. I use ghee when I make this pastry at the restaurant, but butter works well, too. Either way, use the best-quality ghee or butter you can afford. If you don't feel confident flipping the pan over to release the knafeh, leave it in the tin, drizzle with the syrup and serve the pastry straight from the tin.**

⚜ **COOKING TIP** Knafeh freezes beautifully and is very good reheated in an oven (never in a microwave); in fact, it will taste as if you just made it. The unbaked pastry can be frozen, tightly wrapped, for up to 3 months. After it's baked, it will keep in the fridge for 1 week.

Put the shredded dough in a large bowl and pour the melted butter over it. Using your hands, work the dough until it soaks up all the butter. The mixture should feel soft with no dry patches. Divide the dough into two equal parts. It can be tightly wrapped and frozen for up to 1 month.

Preheat the oven to 230°C/gas mark 8. Set out a 45cm round or 30 x 43cm baking tin. If the dough is frozen, hold it in one hand and karate chop it from one end to the other to break it apart. Alternatively, put it into the bowl of a food processor and chop into 3mm pieces.

Pack half of the dough into the tin, evenly spreading it with your hands. Spread the cheese or walnut filling to completely cover the dough. Sprinkle the remaining dough over the filling and, using the palms of your hands, firmly pat down and spread the dough to entirely cover the filling. Take care not to leave any filling exposed (or it will burn) and make sure the dough doesn't touch the edges of the tin (or the knafeh won't release).

Bake until the cheese is entirely melted and the top is golden brown (for the Cheese Knafeh) or the nut filling is hot and the dough is golden brown and crisp (for the Walnut Knafeh), about 20 minutes. While still hot, invert a larger baking sheet or serving platter over the pastry and flip it over to release it. Pour the simple syrup all over the hot pastry. If making the Cheese Knafeh, sprinkle the pistachios all over the top. Cut into 5cm squares or diamonds with a pizza cutter and serve.

MAKES ABOUT 4 DOZEN SQUARES

750g *katayfeh* dough (shredded phyllo)
500g unsalted butter, melted, or ghee
Cheese or Walnut Filling (see opposite)
Simple Syrup (see below), at
    room temperature
250g pistachios, chopped, for garnish
    (for Cheese Knafeh)

MAKING SIMPLE SYRUP

In a saucepan, stir 1.25kg sugar into 2 litres water over medium heat until it boils. Add ½ teaspoon lemon juice, 2 tablespoons orange blossom water and 2 tablespoons rose water. Lower the heat slightly, but continue to boil for 30 minutes. For a thicker syrup, allow to simmer for longer until you've reached the desired consistency. Remove from the heat and let cool. The syrup can be used hot or cold; when using hot syrup make sure the dessert is cold and vice versa. This can be refrigerated in a tightly sealed container for up to one month.

Variation: To add additional pops of flavor consider adding a piece of ginger, orange peel or cloves.

⚜ OLIVES, LEMONS & ZA'ATAR ⚜

CHEESE KNAFEH FILLING

I typically make my own cheese for this when I am preparing it at the restaurant, but it's not necessary if you have access to top-quality cheese curds, ricotta and mozzarella. Cheese curds are often offered at farmers' markets or can be found in specialist cheese shops, some gourmet food shops and online. You can substitute additional mozzarella for the ricotta if you wish.

MAKES ENOUGH FOR ONE 45CM ROUND OR 30 X 43CM KNAFEH

1kg sweet curd cheese
250g ricotta cheese
500g fresh mozzarella cheese, grated

In a large bowl, combine the curd cheese, ricotta and mozzarella and thoroughly mix together. Refrigerate until ready to use.

WALNUT KNAFEH FILLING

This is traditionally made with just walnuts, but I prefer to add almonds and pistachios to the mix. Whatever the combination, use 1.5kg in total.

MAKES ENOUGH FOR ONE 45CM ROUND OR 30 X 43CM KNAFEH

1kg walnuts, chopped
500g whole almonds, or slivered almonds, or pistachios, skinned and chopped
250g raisins or sultanas
250g dessicated coconut
60ml orange blossom water
3 tablespoons rose water (optional)
3 tablespoons vegetable oil
1 teaspoon ground cinnamon
pinch of ground nutmeg
pinch of ground cloves

In a large bowl, combine the walnuts and almonds with the raisins, dessicated coconut, orange blossom water, rose water, if using, oil, cinnamon, nutmeg and cloves. Mix together with your hands until the ingredients are evenly distributed. Set aside until ready to use.

INDEX

ACKNOWLEDGEMENTS

To my daughter and business partner, Jumana, my joy, who stands by me every day at Tanoreen: Your motivation and belief in our family and this book is infinite and I am most grateful.

To my son, Tarek, my light and pride: Your dedication to bringing this book to life was immeasurable, invaluable and appreciated beyond words.

To my husband, Wafa, my partner in life for the last forty years, who has stood by me every step we took on the remarkable road we have shared thus far: I love you.

To Rawda, Azmi, Marwan and Samia, my siblings, whose stories we shared growing up were the basis for this book, and with whom I still cook, eat and stand, together: You bring me great joy.

To my best friends, Yolanda, Soumaya, Suhair and George: We like to eat, and you encouraged me to turn my flourishing passion for cooking into what Tanoreen is today.

To my staff at Tanoreen, who have been loyal for all these years and who helped test endless recipe ideas: Thank you.

To my amazing customers, who supported me from a small ten-table storefront into what Tanoreen has become, and beyond: Many thanks.

Thanks to my team on this book:

Including my writer, Kathleen, for tirelessly reviewing recipe after recipe, working hard and staying motivated this last year.

My agent, Judith, for seeing the light at the end of the tunnel every time.

To our photographer, Pete Cassidy, and Vicki Murrell of Kyle Books, and the family and friends who hosted us abroad at the photo shoot, for bringing every recipe to life and travelling through my childhood with me: Many thanks.

And lastly to my publisher, Kyle, for her vision and confidence in me, and my editor, Anja, whose patience and perspective aligned all the elements together as perfectly as they were meant to be.